contents

you and
your home

what your home means to you

You and the other people you live with are the most important elements in your home. The way you behave, your habits and routines, your likes and dislikes, all have an influence on your living environment. To create a home that is a sanctuary and a haven, you need to decide what it is that makes your ideal home and how that could realistically fit in with your personality. Your home sanctuary is a place for your spirit to rest as well as your taste to be expressed.

Your home is your territory, your personal space, somewhere that you and everyone who lives with you should feel free to be yourselves. It is the one place where you are completely free to express yourself, your hopes, and your dreams. It's also a showcase for who you are, and where your guests can feel at ease and see the best you in your own environment.

The place in which you live should be supportive and nurturing, enabling all of its occupants to deal with the demands of everyday life. It should have an atmosphere that encourages the pursuit of heartfelt ambitions and desires. It is where you go to sleep and where you begin and end each day, so it should be safe, relaxing, and rejuvenating. It should provide a positive platform from which to go out into the world.

Home should not be static though—it should be flexible enough to be lived in, used, and loved. As taste, technology, and the needs of its inhabitants grow and change, your environment should evolve, too. Think of your home as a living thing, an organic whole that develops with you.

But is your home currently all those things? When you think about your home, do you conjure up images of relaxation and enjoyment, or stress and conflict?

keeping a home notebook

To use this book effectively, you should start keeping a notebook. Use it to jot down ideas, take note of colors or patterns that you like, track your own habits, keep a check on prices, and work through some of the exercises in this book. Keeping a notebook should be something you enjoy because it will show the steady progress you make, turning the place you live into a real home sanctuary.

read your home

Someone walking into your home for the first time gets an immediate impression of the kind of person you are and the way you live. The general ambience, the décor, and your sense of organization all create an atmosphere.

In many ways the outside of your home represents the image you give to the outside world. Take a good look at your house from the outside. What do you notice? Does it look well kept and well loved?

As you open the door and come in, what is the first impression you get? Does it smell nice? Does it feel welcoming? Take in the detail and imagine that you are a stranger looking at your home for the first time. What sort of person do you think would be living here? Does it match up with the image you have of yourself?

Take a look around your home right now and think about what it says about you. Does your home reflect who you really are? Or has it somehow ended up saying something quite different? As you move through your house, take in the atmosphere. If you look at your home from a new perspective it is much easier to see how it relates to who you are and to decide what aspects of it you would like to change. Is the place messy or tidy? How does that make you feel? An overly tidy home carries with it a certain tension, but too much chaos is just plain stressful.

The furniture and décor you choose for your home are an important part of the atmosphere you create. Consider your chairs and sofa. Are they more about function or style? Are you attracted to old pine and the comfortable, sociable image that goes with it or to dark, polished wood and the sense of authority and traditional values it represents? Perhaps you have a penchant for antique pieces and you feel an association with a particular period in history, or you have inherited furniture that has a sentimental connection. Maybe you like designer items because they show that you have your finger "on the pulse" or perhaps you prefer to indulge in your own creations and put your own stamp on your home.

Look, too, at the colors you have chosen for your walls, carpets, and furnishings. Are they dark and seductive, bright and uplifting, or cool and soothing? Maybe you've chosen white or cream to give a sense of purity and space. Are the colors you've chosen practical or did you make your decision just because they were visually appealing? Everything in your home represents you and the other occupants in some way. Is your home giving you the image and the feelings that you want it to?

what does my house say?

In your notebook, answer these questions:

1 What kind of person (or people) lives in this place? Make a list of positive and negative adjectives describing this person.

2 Do I like him or her? Be honest but also be kind. There's no point beating yourself up!

3 What is it about this home that makes me reach these conclusions? Be as specific as you can (for example the books in the living room are in alphabetical order, so he must have a lot of time on his hands; the collection of kitchen knives is in top condition, so this person must love to cook…)

4 Do I feel comfortable in this home? Consider this question carefully and if the answer is no, ask yourself why.

you and your home

11

a home for you

Take a look at what you wrote about your home in your notebook under "What Does My House Say?" (page 11). Does the person described there resemble you? In most home decorating books, a lot of emphasis is put on the practical and the aesthetic, but there is another dimension to your home—the spiritual. Your home is a space for your soul as well as your body and your mind. It's a place to house your dreams as well as your old hiking boots and teddy bear. As such, you need to create a comfortable space for your mind, body, and soul, which means getting to know yourself well, and your own strengths and weaknesses as a housekeeper.

How neat am I? Most people like to live in an organized environment because it makes life less complicated and gives them a greater sense of control. Ideally, your home should be organized enough to function well, but also be a place where you can kick off your shoes and relax.

Do I like housework? Some people will never be able to lift a dustpan without experiencing a strange sinking feeling, others have discovered the Zen joy of ironing. You should simply acknowledge how you feel, and try to organize your home accordingly. If you live with others, split the chores between you and plan to make sure that everyone does their fair share. Once you have followed the steps in "Purify Your Home" (pages 46–79), housework may be less of a bore.

Do I own too much stuff? You may find that somehow your possessions have become more powerful than you. You make way for the umbrella stand in the hall and you all squeeze into the living room to watch a giant TV. Your home sanctuary will benefit from less rather than more stuff. Once you have created the right space for yourself, you may find the need to shop less urgent.

What are my habits? Are you an early bird while others in your household are night owls? Do you snack at the refrigerator door or do you sit down to a three-course meal most nights? Go through your household's daily and weekly routines and decide which of your domestic habits is good and which could be changed.

How do I express myself at home? If you haven't got a place at home where you can express who you are—cooking in the kitchen, labeling the shelves in the cupboards and closets, dancing in the dining room, yoga on the bathmat—your frustration will come out somehow. You and everyone else in your household need to be able to feel free to do their thing. This does not necessarily mean hobbies. Think about this idea laterally. When are you at your best? When are you most relaxed?

the best me

List ten things you like about yourself.

List three things you would like to change.

List ten things you love to do.

List three things you loathe (but have to do).

Do the same for each member of the household.

Now think, how can you organize your home so that you make the most of your qualities and change what you want to change; and so that you get to do the things you like more often?

castles in the air

Close your eyes for a few minutes and try to
visualize the home you would love to have. Let your
imagination roam. So it's a beach house in Malibu
with a jacuzzi overlooking the Pacific Ocean—add a
solid pine deck and a little etching by Picasso over
the guest bed. Maybe it's a little hand-built hut by
a Norwegian fjord with a bearskin rug, an open fire,
and Sibelius on the CD player. Be open to any
image that comes to you and revel in your own
fantasy for a while.

In your notebook, describe your fantasy home. If you
like, draw a floorplan. Go into as much detail as you
can. This is not reality, so don't let a tight budget or
a lousy climate hold you back. You are allowed to
live anywhere you want. When you have indulged
yourself to the full, look at what you have written.
What are the most important features of your
fantasy? Is it the open fireplace? Is it the view? Try
to put them in order of importance. Are any of these
ideas achievable now? Could you adapt them to the
place in which you currently live?

your ideal home

To create a home sanctuary, you need to exercise your imagination. This is more important than any amount of money or any number of style magazines. You need to imagine transforming the space you live in now into what you would like it to be. So the first step is to figure out exactly what it is you want. You may surprise yourself. Often our desires are far less extravagant and far more achievable than we think. The only thing that's stopping us is ourselves.

Take a look at the following list of words and, with your home in mind, put them into the order of their importance to you: *comfortable*, *practical*, *beautiful*, *stylish*, *original*, *spacious*, *tranquil*, *social*, *safe*, *relaxing*, *fun*. The first three words you have chosen in the list are most likely to be the three elements you base many of your choices and decisions on when it comes to setting up and altering your home. But what else is important to you?

Answering the questions below will help you become clearer about what you need to make your home a sanctuary. In your notebook, write down your answers in as much detail as you like.

- What impressions would I like to experience when I walk through my front door?
- How would I like others to feel when they come into my home?
- Is a sense of organization important to me?
- Is cleanliness a priority?
- Do I like to invite friends or neighbors over?
- Do I want a home that shows off my originality or creativity?
- Is fashion and style important to me?
- Is having somewhere comfortable to relax important?
- Does my home have to be family or roommate friendly?
- Is privacy a priority?
- Do I need somewhere quiet to meditate/relax/study?
- If I could choose five words to describe my home, what would they be?

one step at a time

You've assessed yourself
and your home. You've
worked out what your
ideal home sanctuary is.
So now it's time to take
some positive steps
towards achieving your
household goals.

In your notebook, make two columns. In column A, list all the things you love, or even just like, about the place you live now. These are the things you want to keep, for example, the sofa, the color scheme, the view. In column B, list all the things you want to change, including you and your family's habits and behavior, for example, the pile of post left on the stairs, the dirt on the kitchen floor, the leftover cooking smells.

Is column A compatible with the home sanctuary that you've written about so far in your notebook? How can you bridge the gap between what you have and what you would like your home to be? If column A is almost empty, that's great, you're starting with a blank slate. If it's full, then you're practically living the dream already.

Put the items in column B in order by priority and affordability. If most of column B is about cleaning and organizing what you already have, you may want to move straight on to "Purify Your Home" (pages 46–79). If there seems to be an overwhelming amount to do, cut the list down to what is realistic. There is nothing more disheartening than a seemingly unachievable list of chores.

Now, read what you've written in your notebook so far, starting right at the beginning. It's time to describe a new fantasy house, but this time one that you can start creating right now. Describe the home you live in (or the home you are moving to) as if it were your ideal home. Make a floorplan and write comments and descriptions.

See what you need to change; it may be very little. Try to keep changes to the actual fabric of your home to a minimum and see what you can improve simply by breaking a habit or doing some dusting or by the addition of some color or a picture.

make a style board

Taking into account all the things you've written in your notebook so far, it's time to create some style boards. These are a great way to focus your ideas. You'll need one or several pieces of corkboard and a handful of thumbtacks. Don't stick anything down permanently. The whole idea of a style board is that you can move things around to see how different colors, textures, and patterns work together.

Start by gathering together pictures of houses, rooms, and gardens that really inspire you. Look for ideas in magazines and books and cut them out or make a color photocopy of any pictures that you feel strongly attracted to. Think in terms of colors that work together and colors that you love. Go into your local furnishing, home improvement, or fabric store and pick out samples that you really like. Think about textures, colors, and patterns. Initially, don't be held back by considerations like cost or space. That will come all too soon.

When you've collected your pictures and samples, stick them onto the boards. Use one board for each room that you intend to tackle. Try arranging your pictures and samples in the general order of the room. For example, position the carpet or flooring you've chosen at the bottom, soft furnishing samples and furniture in the middle, and curtain material or paint colors near the top of the board. This will give you a clearer idea of how the style of the whole room will come together.

Try lining up your style boards in room order and seeing how they work together. Imagine what you see in the picture becoming part of your home and think about whether it would suit the use of the room and would go with the belongings you already have and intend to keep.

get started

Unless you have lots of money and plenty of people to help you, transformation takes time and patience, but if you want to get started right now, try one or more of the following:

1 Think about what your ideal home means to you and decide on three things you can do immediately to make your living environment closer to your ideal. This might be hanging a new picture on the wall or painting your bathroom a different color—do anything that makes you feel positive.

2 Think of just one regular habit or pattern of behavior that prevents you from obtaining your ideal home and make a commitment today to change it. This could be anything from bad money management, which prevents you from buying what you want for your home, to smoking in the living room.

3 Think of one way in which you could give yourself a bit more time to either enjoy or work on your home. You might want to consider getting home earlier from work, for example, or cutting down on your social activities or giving less time to a hobby.

4 If you live with other people, take time today or this week to talk to them about your intentions for your home. See how they feel about it and ask for ideas. If they are positive, find ways in which they can be part of your plan. Maybe you could delegate some of the tasks to them or ask them to help you decorate.

behavior patterns

If you find yourself repeating behavior that seems to hold you back from improving your home, like making your house a mess just after tidying it up or always leaving an home improvement job half finished, you could be stuck in a pattern. We adopt certain patterns throughout our life, picking them up from our parents and friends, or adopting them because they suited us at a particular time, but these patterns may not work for us now. The problem with patterns is that they become so ingrained in our everyday behavior that they begin to subtly run areas of our lives and this is especially recognizable at home. The good news is that patterns are learned behaviors and can therefore be changed. So if you find yourself consistently tripping yourself up at home, spend a day studying your behavior, observe its effects, and take action to change it.

what's stopping you?

If you find yourself making excuses as to why you can't get on with making your home a sanctuary, take a look at the pointers below and see if any of them are holding you back.

Not knowing what you want It is very difficult to get anywhere unless you know what you want to achieve. Without a clear vision of what you want your ideal home to be, you cannot work steadily towards your target.

Procrastination Even when we know what we want from our home, it can take time for us to start moving towards our goal. Maybe you're waiting until you feel differently, have more money, or a new job or relationship—but how long is it going to take? The longer you wait for something to happen, the longer it will take to accomplish your goal. Don't let procrastination get the better of you, start now by doing just one thing in the "Get Started" panel (page 19).

Taking on too much at once Sometimes when we look at where we are now and where we want to be, our goal seems almost impossible to reach. If this is the way you're feeling, break down what you need to do into achievable steps.

Comparing yourself with others When you're looking to improve your home, it's a waste of time comparing yourself with others. No one is the same as you and no one lives life as you do, so adopting someone else's home style is unrealistic. Admiring what they have or how they run their home is something different. If this is the case, put your finger on what it is that you like and see whether it suits you and your household.

Not managing your time and energy One of the biggest problems in our busy lives is trying to fit too much into a limited number of hours. Time management is essential for good housekeeping. If you haven't got a cleaning, cooking, and tidying routine, start one now. Having enough energy is also important, so make sure you allocate time to do tasks when you're not too tired.

Lack of money Not having enough money is something that holds many people back from achieving their dreams. This is often just an excuse, because you may be able to transform your living space simply by instituting a new cleaning regime and moving the furniture. Not everything you need to do with your house will need money, but if you want to buy expensive fixtures and furniture, make a plan and create a budget. This way you will be working towards your goal and even though it may be slow, you will be making progress.

Lack of commitment It is no good just having a desire to create a better home, you also need to have the commitment. This means making a promise to yourself that you will work steadily towards your goal.

enhance
your space

living space

Whether it's a tiny apartment or a Venetian palazzo, your home is basically a space to put things in. The shape and design of that space are factors that you have to take into consideration when you are transforming your home into a sanctuary. Your possessions affect the general dynamic of the space in your home, too. Unless you want to replace any of these items with something more suitable, they should be taken as the basic materials you have to work with when creating your sanctuary. After assessing the current state of your home, there are some simple steps that you can take to make the whole house work better as a unified space.

There's no point pretending your home is a cosy, little miner's cottage in Yorkshire, England, when it's really a spacious brownstone in the city—or vice versa. You need to work with what you have available. Making your home into a sanctuary is a marriage of your ideal home and the real space that you have to work with. A cool, clear assessment of your home—what you like about it and what you hate; what you can change and what's best left alone—is required.

You also need to think about how long you plan to stay in your current home. If you're going to move next year, why waste time and money putting a skylight in the bathroom? A coat of light-colored paint may do a similar job. You should consider what will attract prospective buyers. Their taste might not be the same as yours. However, if this is the home you want to spend a few more years in, then it's worth creating a long-term strategy.

You very well may be able to create your home sanctuary by spending little or no money at all. Before you go out shopping, you need to look at the furniture and accessories that you already have— you could throw away more than you buy.

25

efficiency assessment exercise

The purpose of this exercise is to assess how efficiently your home works. The more smoothly it functions, the more harmonious it will feel. Keep the results of this exercise in mind as you organize the space in each room of your home.

1 Begin by walking around your home and as you look at each area or room, ask yourself the following questions. Can I move comfortably around this area/room or am I navigating an obstacle course? Are there any items on the floor or furniture that could be put on shelves or in cupboards? Are there any items or pieces of furniture that I no longer need or like? Are there any spaces that could be used for storage? Am I making the most of the natural daylight or is something obstructing the windows? Do I have adequate lighting for my needs? Is it too bright? Is this room arranged in the most practical way? Are the items I use most often within easy reach? Does the furniture do its job well?

2 As you move from room to room, ask yourself how easy it is to do so. Pay special attention to the "in-between" spaces in your home. Are they blocked or used as a dumping ground? Is there room for extra storage? Is the style you've chosen in keeping with the style of your house? You don't want to live in a museum, but completely disregarding a building's original features can sometimes damage the spirit of the home. You should be working in sympathy with the fabric of the place.

3 Write the names of each member of your household in your notebook along the top of the page. Under each name write down the activities each person likes to do, how and where they use the house the most. Ask each person how they feel the home could look better and function more efficiently. If the members of your household are old enough, you can ask them to do the list themselves. Take into consideration your lifestyle, your daily routines, and those of the other members of your household. Think about how and where you all cook, eat, communicate, recreate, and relax. How does your home serve your needs? Do you have adequate space to fulfill all of these activities or do some areas need addressing? For example, you might want to consider creating more counter space in the kitchen for a family member who likes to cook, or put aside a quiet area for someone in the household who needs to study. If you have children, maybe you want to find a safe, comfortable place where they can play and toys can be stored away with ease.

create flow

Our homes are an extension of ourselves and, like us, they need to have a healthy energy flow. Another way to describe this energy is to call it the "spirit" or "vitality" of your home. The people and pets in your home, the quality of the air, the smell, light and sounds, the shapes, colors, and textures and the way you use space all affect the spirit of your home and the way its vital energy flows.

Improving and working with the energy flow is not a new idea and has been recognized by various ancient cultures throughout the world for centuries. European pagans, for example, understood the process of space clearing and working with the elements and seasons, while the West African and Mayan shamans made transformations possible by creating sacred space through ritual. More recently, the Chinese practice of feng shui and the Indian practice of vastu shastra have come back into fashion. Both traditions focus on the importance of energy flow and keeping the equilibrium, and both are based on the laws of nature, offering precise methods for manipulating your environment to improve all areas of your life.

However, it isn't necessary to follow a specific school of thought to understand how to improve the flow of energy in your home. Many of the actions you can take, like opening the windows or clearing the clutter, are common sense. Other changes you might want to make are up to your personal taste and how you feel about your environment. Your home is such a unique space that the improvements you make should be connected to your feelings and instincts. If you want to set about improving the spirit of your home right now, try working your way through the following list of actions:

Straighten up The minute your home looks neat and tidy, you should notice a greater feeling of ease.

Clean up Cleaning the surfaces and vacuuming the floor shows that you care about yourself and your environment.

Open the windows Doing this fairly regularly will let stale air out and fresh air in. It not only lifts the atmosphere, but it is also better for your health.

Clear away anything that stops you moving around your home with ease If you find yourself always tripping over shoes or a piece of furniture, do something about it. Part of having a good

common energy stoppers

Mess

Dirt

Stale air

Bad odors

Décor that needs updating

Broken objects

Uncomfortable furniture

Unwelcoming colors and designs

atmosphere in your home is being able to move around freely.

Take time to get to know your favorite colors and styles, and bring them into your home If you choose décor that makes you feel good, you will naturally lift the atmosphere.

Make sure your furniture is comfortable If you have comfortable beds, dining room chairs, and living room furniture, you will find it much easier to rest, eat, and relax, creating a more satisfying environment.

Add something living to the atmosphere like a plant or fresh flowers Plants and flowers will add their own positive energy to your home. Plants are particularly beneficial because they can improve the quality of the air.

Create an aroma you love Make some fresh coffee, buy a bunch of flowers, or spray your home with your favorite essential oil. You will find that the right aroma gives your home an instant lift.

Do something in your home that makes you feel happy Watch your favorite movie, invite a group of friends around, or have a luxury bath. Do something that anchors good feelings to your home.

rules for room arrangement

Figuring out the best way to arrange a room is tricky—even the professionals usually have to try a few ways before getting it right. But if you have a lot of furniture or possessions, a limited amount of space or an unevenly shaped room, finding just the right disposition of objects can seem almost impossible. Sometimes, the problem is that you bought your furniture for one home and now that you have moved, it just does not fit. If you move your furniture around and find it still doesn't work, try again. You will eventually find the best way or you could opt to exchange it for something different.

Always keep in mind the smooth flow of energy when you're arranging a room. Feng shui practitioners suggest that you don't want energy to move too quickly through an empty space, or too slowly in an overcrowded room. There are a number of basic rules you can follow which will help.

Know the traffic patterns One of the most important elements to laying out a room well is understanding the traffic patterns. These are the spaces where people need to move through the room. Starting at the door, look at where people are most likely to walk through the room. Take into consideration the need to access bookshelves, drawers, the stereo and television, windows, and exits. You don't want too much traffic right through the main seating area of your living room for instance.

Find the focus Most rooms have at least one focal point. This could be a fireplace, a work of art, an attractive window, or a special piece of furniture, say a double bed. Arrange the room around the focal point. Think how your eye travels around the room. Does the arrangement flow in an aesthetically pleasing way? You may want to use color to create points of interest that connect the space—for example, bright cushions along a pale sofa leading to a colorful painting, then over to a vase on the mantelpiece, and down to a strongly colored armchair.

Create balance Often rooms are easier on the eye when they give the impression of being balanced. You can achieve this quite simply by having two matching objects in the room, for example two lamps, or two candlesticks. You can also achieve this more subtly by using objects of a similar size and/or color—say, a red armchair and a blue one.

Cluster furniture Furniture, especially in the living and dining rooms, should be placed close enough together to allow people to see each other and hold a conversation with ease. People often make the mistake of pushing furniture up against a wall when it would be better to allow traffic to flow behind the piece.

questions to ask yourself when arranging a room

1 What are the functions of this room?

2 How often do I plan to use this room?

3 How many people will be using the room?

4 Who is going to be using the room?

5 What do I want to display and store in this room?

6 What is my ideal floor covering?

7 What kind of lighting do I need in this room?

8 Is there any furniture I need to add to this room?

9 What electrical equipment do I need in this room?

10 How can I arrange this room so that it pleases me?

create space

If your house or flat is feeling
overwhelmed and claustrophobic,
use these ideas to create a feeling
of spaciousness. Even the biggest
area can sometimes feel cramped
simply because of the way things
are arranged. These ideas also help
with the general flow of energy
and allow your home to "breathe."

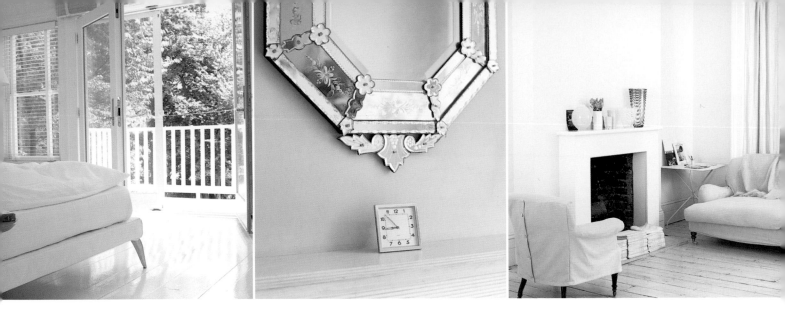

Eliminate obstructions The further you can see through a space, the larger and more open it will seem. Whenever possible, arrange your furniture so that it leaves plenty of floor exposed and avoid blocking views to windows and doors.

Use lighter colors Lighter colors make a room look bigger and, if you want to keep the space uncomplicated, opt for matching or complementary furnishings.

Bring in more light Expand the size of your space by allowing in as much natural light as possible and adding additional light fixtures.

Use mirrors Mirrors reflect light and add space to a room. Make sure you place them opposite something attractive like a window, a painting, or your favorite piece of furniture.

Go for open plan If you live in a small space and have the option, knocking down walls and opening up rooms will give you a greater feeling of space and light. If you have an open plan room but need some temporary privacy between spaces, folding doors or screens can be very useful.

Build in furniture where you can You will save space if you can build in furniture like bookshelves, desks, and cupboards to fit the precise dimensions of the space available.

Choose furniture with care A few carefully chosen pieces of furniture rather than lots of smaller pieces of furniture make a room look bigger. If you don't have room for full-scale armchairs or sofas, an upholstered armless style will still provide the comfort but allow more space.

Opt for multifunction furniture In small spaces, choosing furniture that can multitask will save you space. Small sofas that can fold into beds are great space savers and high beds that have enough room for a desk or wardrobe beneath them double your usable space.

Keep décor simple Complicated designs overwhelm, so keep fabrics and furnishings like curtains, carpets, wallpaper, and furniture coverings simple. Emphasize a sense of space by covering sofas and chairs with plain or textured upholstery rather than complex patterns.

Keep flooring continuous Keeping the same flooring material throughout the house gives a sense of continuity and space.

Take advantage of outdoor space Stretch your living space by making the views from windows, balconies, or patios more accessible.

a tour of your home

Now it's time to take a serious tour of your house, thinking about how it works as a unified whole and how the rooms work individually. Think about the blocks of space created by walls and furniture in each room. Are they awkwardly shaped? Apply all the ideas you have already learned in this chapter to each room. As you walk around, make notes in your book.

the outside

Realtors know better than anyone the importance of the front of a dwelling—most people make up their mind about a potential buy within 15 to 30 seconds of seeing it. The entrance to your home—front door, steps, garden, or driveway—is like an introduction into your world, and it is the means by which you and others make a transition from the public realm into your personal space.

We often assume that everyone wants the front of their house to be welcoming—but this is not necessarily the case. If you live in a bad neighborhood, it might be quite a good idea to put people off. Alternatively, you may be a very private person. You must decide how you want your entrance to work.

You already have some idea of your ideal home—how does the front of your house or apartment show this? Is there any correspondence between your ideal and the reality? If you live in a small apartment with a scruffy front door but your ideal home is rather grand, ask yourself what you can do to bridge the gap between reality and fantasy. What about painting the front door a shiny black and replacing the door knob and knocker?

Feng shui experts also consider the front of the house to be of great importance, believing that the front door is where the majority of "chi," or energy, enters your home. Keeping the entrance clear and well presented is said to welcome in new opportunities and money. If you feel your front door is dreary, polish the door handle and trim and clean the front steps. You may want to consider fixing a good outside light. Also make sure that your doorbell works.

colors

The color you choose for your front door makes a statement about who you are.

Natural wood A no-nonsense approach to life.

Dark blue Practical and authoritative.

Black Serious and aloof.

White A desire for perfection.

Yellow Sociable and lively.

Pink Nurturing and welcoming.

Purple An individualist.

numbers

The number of your home is said to have an influence on your life. Pythagoras, one of the great philosophers and mathematicians of Ancient Greece, is understood to be the founder of numerology. He believed that the whole universe was ordered mathematically and that each number, especially the numbers from one to nine, exerted a particular influence over our lives. If your home number is more than one digit, you will need to add the digits together until you get a single number. For example, if your house number is 356, you need to add together 3+5+6=14, then add together 1+4=5. So your house number would be 5.

if your house number is:	
1	*Expect to live an independent and individual existence in this home. You may find yourself called on to be a leader in some way.*
2	*This is a home best shared with someone else. You should find it easy to express your feelings, but may feel lost if you don't have a partner.*
3	*This is an ideal house in which to work on a creative project, study, or enjoy a good social life. Romance should thrive in this location as long as you treat it with respect.*
4	*This home should provide a good solid foundation for a family home. It is an excellent number if you want to bring a sense of order and structure into your life.*
5	*This is a great home for people who don't like to be pinned down to a routine. It's particularly good if you are impulsive or like variety.*
6	*This is a wonderful house for love and harmony, especially if you have children or pets. However, too much importance placed on possessions could create discord.*
7	*This is a house with a feeling of privacy, which is good for spending time alone to learn and study. There may be a desire for perfection and elegance.*
8	*This is a wonderful home for working towards a goal. A feeling of authority and respect for the community influences this home.*
9	*This is a house for learning about humanity. It may create a number of changes and experiences for the inhabitants.*

public spaces

Unless you live in a studio apartment, your home probably divides naturally into public and private spaces—and for most of us it's important to keep the atmosphere and ambience of these two parts of the home different. Conversation pieces that we happily display in the living room may be wasted in the bedroom—and a loving portrait of your granny may be lost in the living room but just right on a dressing table.

Your public spaces are not only where you are on show but also where you have to share with the rest of the household. Public spaces also tend to be high-traffic areas. You need to be able to move around them easily and you need to take into account wear and tear.

Naturally, these are the areas where most compromise is necessary, but there's no reason why they have to end up an aimless mishmash of things. You can make people's differing needs work together.

the front entrance

The entrance of your home should be given special care and attention since it's the first place seen by you and other people upon entering your home. Most people want their entrance to be warm and welcoming and the right lighting, attractive pictures, and well-chosen colors will all encourage this. Bear in mind that some visitors may see only this part of your living environment, so it should give the right impression.

Always remember that the main function of the front entrance is to allow people to enter and leave your home, so it should be free of obstacles and the décor ought to be easy to look after. A good door mat inside and outside the front door cuts down on grime.

There are other functions of the front entrance that you need to consider, too. The front door is sometimes the place where the mail comes in, so you need somewhere to put your unopened mail. You'll also need a place to hang hats and coats, and maybe leave shoes and umbrellas.

halls, landings, and staircases

In-between spaces can be a challenge to use well. First and foremost, they are designed as traffic routes to allow people to move from one area of the house to another, so this must always remain the priority. As with all high-traffic areas, halls, landings, and stairs need to be furnished with materials that are durable and easy to clean. Safety is always a priority here so make sure these areas are well lit and clear of clutter. If you often find toys, magazines, or other items on the stairs, get a stair basket that is shaped to fit steps and can be used as short-term storage.

However, your in-between spaces do not have to be uninteresting or left as wasted space. With careful consideration they can be used for other purposes, too—whether it's storing books in the hall, putting up shelves above doors or finding space for a hidden bathroom under the stairs. Even small halls and landings can be used as miniature picture galleries or compact libraries. Paperbacks can be stored on wall-hung bookshelves in any of these areas if space allows, since they don't demand particularly deep shelves. If you want to make the space appear larger, painting the walls a lighter color or using a well-placed mirror will help.

living room

The living room is one of the most important rooms in the house. It's the place to spend time relaxing, talking, and entertaining, so you should spend time and effort getting it just right. Often we have too much or too little furniture in here, making it feel squashed or uncomfortable. Check to see whether your arrangement follows the guidelines in "Rules for Room Arrangement" (pages 30–31). Is your furniture comfortable? Try sitting in each seat and see how it feels. Does your furniture work well together? Choosing colors that complement each other or opting for matching cushions and throws will help create a sense of harmony.

Does your living room have a focal point—other than the television? It should be something beautiful, fascinating, or soothing—perhaps a fireplace, a work of art, or a view. Check to see whether your lighting is doing its job. It should be warm and intimate but at the same time there should be some seats with light that is good enough to read by.

dining room

Dining rooms are often reserved for eating, although with a shortage of space in many homes, dining rooms often double up as an office or a hobby room. Is your dining room table clear of clutter? Can you have your meals here efficiently and comfortably?

kitchen

Whether your taste is trendy stainless steel or cosy farmhouse, your kitchen is often the heart of your home. It is probably is somewhere we congregate for a chat. However, for most of us, the first function of the kitchen is cooking and storing food. This is the moment to think about just how you use this space. Is everything stored in the most sensible place? Are the things you use easy to access? Are your cupboards well organized? Is there any wasted space? If you're thinking of completely revamping the kitchen, think about your pattern of movement between sink, stove, storage, and counter.

kitchen tips

There are some simple steps you can take to make your kitchen work more efficiently. Arrange your utensils, such as cutting boards, knives, and mixing bowls near to where you use them. Be clever about finding new storage space. Putting a hinge on kickboards (the boards at the bottom of floor units) creates a whole new storage area for baking trays. To keep your kitchen surfaces clear, find new ways to store your equipment—such as ceiling hangers for saucepans or hooks for cups. Make sure your kitchen is well lit without being harshly bright. Make sure your kitchen wastebasket is handy to get to and, lastly, have flooring that's easy to clean.

enhance your space

private spaces

The private rooms in your home are where your imagination can work freely— somewhere you can nurture your dreams. Check to see whether you have taken full advantage of your private spaces. You should feel completely relaxed here and totally at peace with your surroundings.

bedroom—your personal sanctuary

One of the greatest gifts you can give yourself is a bedroom where you can totally relax and shut out the world. Unless you have a dressing room, you are likely to keep your clothes, shoes, and other personal belongings in the bedroom, so good storage that is easy to access is a top priority for your bedroom.

It's worth spending money on a decent bed—adults spend almost one-third of their lives in bed. Lie on it and see whether it's really comfortable. Your bed should be a focal point of your bedroom, so choose attractive covers.

children's bedrooms

For children, the bedroom is not only a place to sleep, but also a playpen and a study. They easily create a sea of toys so storage that is simple to get to and will encourage your children to pick up is key.

study or workroom

If you are lucky enough to have your own room in which to work or pursue your hobby, you should make absolutely sure that it is laid out in a way that optimizes its functions. The same applies to any study areas within other rooms in your home. The chair should support your back. The desk should be at the right height to support your wrists if you work on a computer. Books, computer equipment, tools, and any other accessories should be easily accessible and neatly stored. This may be only the tiniest of spaces, so you need to keep it shipshape, and that means a place for everything and everything in its place. It's worth getting specific storage for speciality hobbies and, if space is tight, consider wall-mounted drawers and small shelves.

bathroom

Bathrooms can be both public and private spaces. Consider what it's like from a guest's point of view. Is it clean and inviting? If you share your home, your bathroom may be something of a crossroads with traffic jams in the morning and evening. Is there any way you can ease the congestion? You should allocate space for each person's belongings, so that they know just what areas should be kept tidy.

10 things you can do right now

Enhancing the space in your home is not just a matter of straightening up and reshuffling your furniture. It's about taking a look at where and how you live and making time to think about how you can arrange your living space to enhance the quality of your life. Start by improving the space that you live in right now by trying one or more of the following.

1 Brighten up the front of your home by giving your door and the surrounding area a good clean. Create a more attractive exterior by adding a large potted plant, a hanging basket, or a window box filled with flowering plants.

2 Part of having a relaxing atmosphere in your home is being able to move around with ease. So have a look at the high-traffic areas in your home and clear away anything that creates an obstacle.

3 Take a look at and try out the furniture that you, your family, and your guests use the most. How comfortable is it? Pay particular attention to your chairs, sofas, and beds. Is there anything you can add to them to make them more comfortable, for example pillows or new upholstery?

4 Connect your home to positive feelings and memories by choosing a symbol that represents your favorite place to be. This could be a shell from a beach you love to visit, a painting of your favorite woodlands, or a holiday photograph of yourself having fun. Place it somewhere that you will see it often.

5 Give your home a breath of fresh air by opening the windows to let the air circulate for a while. Place house plants around your home to improve the quality of air and add life to the atmosphere.

6 Take a look around your home and think of three ways in which you can improve the way your home functions. For example, would it help to clear a bigger space for cooking? Maybe you could arrange your bedroom so that the clothes and possessions you use most often are the handiest, or perhaps you could improve the quality of the lighting in one of the rooms to better suit your needs.

7 Choose two rooms that you use frequently, like the living room and bedroom, and decide on the focal point of each room, for example an attractive window, a fireplace, a bed, or a picture. Once you've chosen your focus, arrange the furniture accordingly.

8 Get rid of or replace one possession that you really don't like or use very often. If you can choose something that you have had to look at every day, the improvement will be more obvious.

9 Think of different ways of creating an environment that better represents the personalities of everyone who lives in your home. You might want to choose particular colors, pictures, or ornaments that mean something special to each of you.

10 Bring pleasant feelings into your home by doing something that makes you feel happy. This could be watching a favorite film, holding a dinner party, or enjoying a good soak in the bath.

purify your home

good housekeeping

Your home may already be
perfectly decorated and ideally
designed, but in order to create
a real sanctuary, you also need
to keep the place running
smoothly. This means doing
three things: straightening up,
cleaning, and organizing.

Having a good clear out, letting go of what you don't want, and finding a place for those items you want to keep is a good place to start if you want to improve the state of your home. It will not only help to cut down on the time you spend searching for things you have mislaid, but also reduce the time you spend cleaning and straightening up. Giving your home a thorough clean will give you a fresh start and help you keep up the good work you've already achieved. Finally, you will need to give your habits an overhaul and adopt a method of organization that will allow you to stay in control of your wonderful revamped home.

Before you embark on any home transformation, devote some thought to what makes you happy and puts you at ease when it comes to your home. Create a vision of the end result you would like to achieve. Imagine what it would be like to have a home that functions well and runs smoothly. If you haven't already done so, you may want to write down your ideas in your notebook. Make your vision compelling and exciting. What will you have room for in your life when you are free of the clutter that is holding you back? What will it be like to be able to find things when you want them? How will it feel to have a perfectly clean home? Will it feel good to make a favorable impression on others when they enter your home? Make your vision as real as you can—it is this image of a wonderful home that will drive you on to achieve your goals and keep you motivated.

As with any big task, it's best to take an overall view of the job ahead, then break it down into small assignments that are easy to achieve, so that you are heartened by each result and feel inspired to keep going. So take your notebook and, using a different page for each room, head three columns: Straightening up, Cleaning and Organizing. Write the name of the room you are dealing with above the headings. Then walk around your home making a note under each column of where your clutter, cleaning, and disorganization problems lie in each room. Take a particular note of whether you feel nourished or drained by what you see, which rooms need the most attention, and where in the house your biggest clutter hotspots and neglected cleaning duties lie.

This is now your task list, but don't feel you have to complete it all at once. As you clean, straighten up, and reorganize each area on your list, tick it off and give yourself a reward commensurate with the effort involved. So for an easy task, for example, you could allow yourself a chocolate eclair and for a really time-consuming, emotionally draining one, buy some tickets to the theater. Giving yourself a treat will help you to keep up the good work.

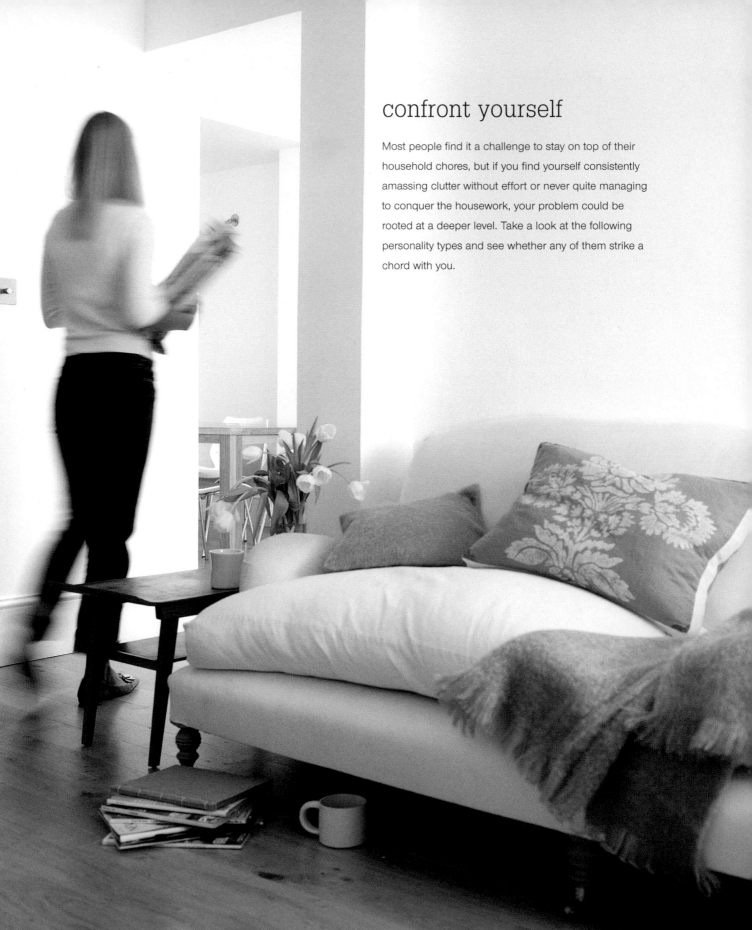

confront yourself

Most people find it a challenge to stay on top of their household chores, but if you find yourself consistently amassing clutter without effort or never quite managing to conquer the housework, your problem could be rooted at a deeper level. Take a look at the following personality types and see whether any of them strike a chord with you.

the hoarder

Hoarders tend to keep most things, with the belief that they may be useful one day. Cupboards, shelves, attics, and garages are full of old stuff that the hoarder has never felt able to let go of—"just in case."

The sad thing is that many of the items a hoarder holds onto never actually get used, and instead their home becomes more and more bogged down with stuff. This behavior is often rooted in insecurity—hoarders hold onto things because they fear they may not have what they need when the time comes. This can be a very practical view in times of scarcity, but nowadays material possessions, packaging, and junk mail come into our lives with such ease that a clearing out strategy is essential if any home is to function well.

If hoarding is your problem, you need to remind yourself that if you let go of what you don't need, you make space for what you do need and want. Life will become simpler, you'll have more time and less stuff to get in your way. If you find it difficult to let go of things because you hate waste, think about your unwanted items going to good homes where they will be used. You can also look at ways of recycling, whether it's cardboard, packaging, or old electrical items, instead of letting clutter clog up your life.

the deferrer

Deferrers often have piles of paperwork, videos, photographs, and all sorts of other possessions just waiting to be sorted and organized. Guilty of putting off today what they can do tomorrow, deferrers come in two guises: the "perfectionist deferrer" and the "lazy deferrer." The former puts off jobs until they have time to do it properly and if they tend to be short of time, the task never gets done. "Lazy deferrers" just can't get themselves motivated and so ignore the situation until it gets out of hand. Bills that need paying, letters that need answering, items that need cleaning or repairing, ironing and other household chores are all set aside to be dealt with another day.

If this is you, you need to remind yourself that action does pay off and the sooner you get your chores done, the quicker you'll create guilt-free time to do those things you really enjoy. Since this behavior is grounded in procrastination, the answer is to take action. For some deferrers, simply making a start creates the energy and motivation they need to keep going, but for most deferrers, they need a bit more of a push and could do with a friend to help.

the rebel

Rebels are often surrounded by mess—clothes strewn around the house, old food packaging in the kitchen and a bathtub that's never cleaned. Rebels find it hard to get themselves to do such boring activities as putting their clothes away, doing the dishes, or the vacuuming. Even if they would like to live in a presentable home, they see straightening up, cleaning, and organizing as conforming to rules and regulations that just don't appeal to them. Sometimes rebels come from equally rebellious families where they learned to question and rebel against authority and rules, and sometimes they come from families where they were forced to straighten up and keep clean as children, and they still resent it.

If this is you, you need to think about how your rebelliousness is interfering with what you want in your life. Remind yourself that you are not carrying out chores because you want to conform to someone else's rules, but because it helps you achieve your goals, by allowing your life to run more smoothly. If you come from a rebellious family, look at how you could improve on the habits you were taught. If your problem stems from being bossed around as a child, tell yourself that you are the adult now and acknowledge that you decide what you want to do and what you need to do—then do it.

the sentimentalist

Sentimentalists often have a home full of knick-knacks, ornaments, soft toys, letters, cards, and all sorts of other mementoes. Like the hoarder, the sentimentalist suffers from insecurity. At the root of most sentimentalism is the desire or need to hold onto the past, with each memento treasured for its connection to a particular period in their life. Sentimentalists often fear that if they let go of a particular item or possession, the memory will disappear with it and so everything is kept—from old school papers, to out-of-date greetings cards—even if they are never looked at again.

If this is you, you need to remind yourself that whether or not you keep your mementoes, the memory still remains. If you want something to connect you to a particular memory or person, keep the special items that have the strongest connections, like a favorite photograph or an important letter, or write down the events in a special diary. There is no need to keep everything. If you have a pile of your children's drawings, or loads of soft toys, keep a selection of the best and let the rest go, so that you have room for the new things to come in. Remind yourself that the past is gone, that your life right now is more important and that you have a future ahead with more good times and positive memories to come.

half-finished tasks

You may have a raft of reasons for not finishing a task that you have set out to do—but most of these reasons come down to bad planning. Take a look at this list and see whether any of these ring a bell.

1 Attempting to do too much at once.

2 Lack of setting clear goals and deadlines.

3 Running out of time.

4 Changing priorities halfway through a task.

5 Not having the right organizational tools available, for example bags, boxes, and storage facilities.

6 Loss of interest in the task.

straighten up

Living a neat, organized
life must be a conscious
decision. Keeping your
home in the best state
possible means you must
stay aware of what is
going on around you and
to be mindful of how
your actions affect your
surroundings. Take note
of any habits that create
clutter, for example
leaving your coffee mug
beside the bed in the
morning, not cleaning
the bathtub when you've
finished, and leaving the
top off the toothpaste.

In your notebook, you have a list of the messiest areas of your home. Start by tackling the easiest. Keep mess to a minimum by following these simple guidelines.

Learn to recognize clutter Whether it's junk mail, a bad purchase, or a present that you dislike, learn to recognize clutter as soon as it enters your house and you will soon cut your clutter down to size.

Be aware that most material items can be replaced, but your time can't Your time is precious and far more important than your possessions. When you feel hesitant or guilty about letting go of possessions, think how often you waste your time buying, straightening up, and being concerned about possessions that don't really matter in the bigger scheme of life.

Attack the worst hotspots in your home first Stuff like books, videos, clothes, and paperwork tends to pile up in particular areas. If you choose the worst hotspots to clear first, you will notice the results immediately and the smaller muddles around your home will be a breeze to conquer.

Be prepared before starting a task Before you start clearing clutter, gather together everything you'll need to complete the task. For example, make sure you have the right boxes and bags. Maybe you'll need labels and pens or a basket to put things in. Being prepared will stop you having to wander off to look for things while you work, which could lead you to being distracted and never finishing the job.

Keep motivated by working in short bursts
If you find it difficult to stay motivated, work for 15 minutes at a time, then give yourself a break. It may take longer overall to get your task done but you'll be more likely to complete the task.

Learn to stay on top of your clutter Once you have cleared the backlog of mess, set aside 5 to 10 minutes a day to put things back in their place and sort out any new clutter. This will save you time, space, and energy in the long run and help you to stay organized.

Fix things Instead of leaving broken china to gather dust on a shelf, or shirts with missing buttons in your closet, get them mended —or do it yourself.

sentimental clutter

To make our house a home, we need some sentimental belongings, but the problem comes when we have too many. Out of all the clutter we own, the hardest to part with is probably the sentimental stuff. These are items that we keep because they allow us to connect to people or situations in the past. Letting go of personal memorabilia can be hard, especially if the situation to which it is connected was emotionally important.

Sometimes we hang onto things after a trauma and find it difficult to move on. On other occasions clutter provides a useful distraction from thinking about the deeper issues in our lives. Hoarding sentimental items often leads us to become stuck in the past, which prevents us from moving on and making the most of our lives.

If you feel that sentimental clutter is one of your biggest problems, try the suggestions from the list below. If, after you've tried these guidelines, you still feel stuck, it may be healing to seek professional help and find out how to get to the core of the problem.

Sift out the sentimental items Gather together all the things you think you're keeping for sentimental reasons.

The choice is yours Don't feel obliged to get rid of anything that you don't want to. Ultimately the choice is yours, so don't bother to justify your choices or make excuses. Just let go of those things you feel ready to relinquish.

Save the best If you have a choice of items with a similar sentimental connection, choose the best to keep and let the rest go. Sort out those items that have a real personal connection and history from those that don't.

Enlist the support of close friends and family If you feel unsure about which items to keep or let go, get someone you trust to help you decide.

Make space for your mementoes Make sure your mementoes have somewhere to live. Save only those you have space for.

Keep the mementoes that make you happy Go through your mementoes and ask yourself how you feel about each one. If any of them make you feel sad or bad in any way, ask yourself why you are keeping them.

Organize and cut down on your mementoes by arranging them in a scrapbook or journal or by placing them in a specially chosen box If you want to let something go, but still want a connection to it, make a record of it in your journal—it will help you keep the memories fresh, but let go of the clutter.

Give yourself time Don't let go of sentimental clutter until you're ready to or you may worry about whether you've done the right thing. Have a "decisions box" in which to keep your undecided sentimental clutter and review it every now and again when you're in the mood. If items sit in your "decision box" for a long time without you noticing or thinking about them, ask yourself whether you really need the items or would miss them if you let them go.

tackle the paper mountain

One of the most time-consuming and common clutter hotspots in many homes are paper piles. Letters, bills, bank statements, catalogs, and junk mail land on the doormat almost daily, workbags explode with papers, and children come home from school armed with artwork and notices. It's no wonder that keeping control of paperwork is a challenge in most homes. A useful tip is to have a special notebook or pad for notes, messages, and lists to prevent writing on scraps of paper all over the house. Once the book is full, you can transfer any useful information into address books, calendars, or scrapbooks and throw it out if you choose.

Paper clutter costs time, energy, and sometimes money, and without an organized plan, a household can drown in a rising inflow of paper. So if you're struggling, take control. Set aside some time every day to do your paperwork. Have a wastepaper basket beside you as you work, and your diary or calendar and address book handy. Put paperwork that needs action, such as bills, letters, and any other mail that needs a response in a special tabletop file or folder. Have another file for material that you intend to read. Anything that should be kept ought to be filed immediately.

To stop accumulating drifts of paper, you should decide what to do with each piece of paper as soon as it lands in your hands.

- Set aside some time each day to keep your paperwork and files organized.
- When the mail arrives, immediately get rid of anything you don't want or need. In addition to the obvious junk mail, get rid of the ads that accompany bills and magazines, as well as the envelope. Sort the remaining mail into categories like letters, bills, magazines, newspapers, and catalogs, ready to be put in the right place.
- When the latest issue of a magazine comes in, recycle the previous issue. If you want to save them for awhile, have a basket or magazine holder to put them in. Create a rule that you will only save as many magazines as will fit in the basket or holder.
- Keep any important schedules on a bulletin board.
- Read your newspapers daily and recycle them afterwards. If there is an article that you don't have time to read, cut or tear it out and put it into a reading file. If you have a great pile of these to read through, break them down into small sections. You can then read these smaller piles each day—on the bus or train to work, in the bath, in bed in the evening, or at any other time that is convenient to you.

paper clutter-busters

A filing cabinet This is where you should file everything that needs to be kept in the long term. Each drawer should be equipped with labeled hanging folders. You can organize your folders alphabetically, but it is often better to make sure that you place the most frequently used files near the front of the drawer and the less frequently used ones near the back.

Storage boxes These are essential for bulky paperwork like old tax information, which you don't want to put or can't fit into your filing cabinet, but you still need to keep.

your closet

Arranging your clothes well can make a significant difference to how you look and feel. Typically, we tend to wear 20 percent of our clothes 80 percent of the time, so it's the other 80 percent of your clothes that need to undergo careful scrutiny. Before you get started, it's important that you decide how much uninterrupted time you can spare. To clear out your closet and clothes drawers, a large chunk of time is better than small sessions if you can manage it, since it's better to complete the task in one go. If you have a lot of clothes, you may decide to take three sessions: closet, drawers, and then shoes. You'll need bags or boxes ready to pack the clothes for the thrift store, reselling, or recycling.

- Take everything out of your closet and drawers and put it on your bed.
- Give your closet and drawers a thorough clean.
- Put back those clothes, shoes, and bags that you love and wear or use.
- Let go of anything that doesn't suit you in either style or color or that is made from fabric you don't like.
- If anything that you want to keep needs mending or sending to the dry cleaners, vow to sort it out when you've finished.
- Try on the items that are left, deciding whether they look and feel good. Ask yourself whether you can imagine yourself wearing these clothes or shoes again, whether they suit you and whether you really want them. If you haven't worn these items over the last couple of years, will you wear them again?
- If you have clothes or shoes that you are not sure about, put them to one side and give yourself a few weeks to think about them. If you can, wear them during this time to see how they feel.
- When you've finished, group similar items together. Then put them in order of seasons and colors. For example, winter dresses should be grouped together and then similar colors put together within these groupings.
- Make sure each item of clothing has a place and make sure the clothes you wear most often are handiest.

be clothes conscious

There are three reasons why you could be hanging onto clothes unnecessarily: guilt, a change in your size, or sentimentality.

You feel guilty about letting them go Guilt often crops up when we've spent a lot of money on an outfit that is inappropriate in some way or we were given clothes as a present. Either way, if you are not going to wear them, it's not worth keeping them. Get over your guilt by giving them to someone who will appreciate them.

You're waiting until you lose weight Be realistic, are you really going to lose enough weight to get into this outfit or is it just going to clog up your closet? If you do seriously intend to lose enough weight to get into it, set yourself a deadline and do it.

You feel this outfit has sentimental connections Outfits you wore on special occasions will usually hold memories for you, in which case you might want to keep them, but be selective. Know why you are keeping the outfit and what you intend to do with it. For example, do you intend to save your wedding dress for your daughter when she gets married or would you be better off making an evening dress out of the material, so that your wedding dress is still being worn and not wasted. Keep only those clothes that have strong sentimental connections and let the others go.

practical cleaning

Household cleaning can feel like a
never-ending chore, but with planning
and a regular routine, the effort you
need to stay on top of the housework
can be greatly reduced.

Some people are natural cleaners, who can't go to bed or leave the house until every chore is done while others just can't seem to get themselves motivated to accomplish even the smallest task. If you recognize yourself in the latter, you need to take yourself in hand and start introducing some helpful habits.

Part of staying on top of housework is also about preventing build up. This means that you should clean up after yourself, straighten the kitchen after each meal, clean the tub after you've used it, and generally restore your home back to its clean and orderly state as you go through the day.

Having a routine may sound boring, but it is the successful way to achieve a clean and tidy house. You may choose to do all your cleaning on the same day, but it's probably easier to do a few chores every day. Try having a weekly schedule, for example, Monday is laundry day, Tuesday is cleaning the kitchen day, and so on. If you share your home with others, instigate a rota. This may not be popular at first, but once everyone gets used to it, having a rota means everyone knows what they're doing so there's less room for argument.

daily tasks

Open the windows to let fresh air circulate This will create a healthier environment, cut down on humidity and reduce the number of dust mites.

Clean surfaces In the kitchen, let your cleaning product soak up the grime on the stovetop while you wipe down the surfaces, tiles, sink, and faucets, then go back to the stove afterwards to make the job easier.

Air the beds Allowing air to get to your mattress will cool the bed down and discourage dust mites.

weekly tasks

Straighten up Having clear floors, seats, and surfaces is essential if you want to do a fast and full clean up. If you don't have time to put things away before you start cleaning, have a basket ready to put everything in from each room.

Clean toilets, bath, shower, and sinks, and wash down the tiles Spray your toilet cleaner around the bowl and let it soak in while you get on with cleaning the bath, shower, and sink. Then return to the toilet and give it a

good clean. A cup of baking soda poured down the toilet once a week is great for neutralizing odors and preventing blockages.

Change the towels Wash your towels at 140°F (60°C).

Put out the trash and sort out the recycling Make sure that the trash always goes out before the garbagemen come, otherwise your garbage may be hanging around for up to a week outside your house. When it comes to recycling, it helps to have somewhere to store your recycling during the week.

Wipe down doors, cupboard handles, and appliances Everyone in the house tends to use the doors, handles, and appliances leaving dirty hand marks and germs, so make sure you use hot soapy water and a clean cloth to prevent bacteria being spread around.

Change the bedding Wash your bed linen at 140°F (60°C).

Sort out your laundry If you want to feel the full benefits of your clean clothes and linen, make sure you hang out the laundry or put it in the dryer the same day that you wash it.

Shake out and rearrange your cushions and throws Plumping up the seats and cushions and straightening the throws is a speedy way to give your living room a fresh look.

Dust Start with the higher shelves and surfaces and move downwards. Make sure you do the dusting before cleaning the

floors so that the dust gets cleaned up. A slightly damp duster will help you collect dust instead of dispersing it, but make sure you rinse it out thoroughly as you go.

Vacuum the floors Vacuuming should always be done after most of the dirty jobs have been finished, so that you can vacuum up any dirt or dust left over. Once you have clear floors it is often easier to vacuum the whole house doing one room after the other, instead of stopping and starting.

Clean the floors If you have wooden, tiled, or laminate floors you need to sweep up or vacuum the crumbs and dirt before cleaning the floor. Make sure you have a mop for the bathroom and a mop for the kitchen.

monthly tasks

If you've been following your daily and weekly routine your home should be looking good. But there are some chores that need to be done only once a month or so. Nevertheless these are real essentials. As with the weekly chores, it's best if you have a schedule and a rota. Don't be frightened off because that sounds like work. Being organized means less work in the long run—and more time for fun.

Turn the mattresses This will help to air the mattresses and encourage them to recover their shapes. If your mattress smells musty, sprinkle baking soda on top, leave for at least an hour, then vacuum off.

Clean the windows and mirrors You may not need to or have time to clean all of your windows every month, so choose a couple of windows to do at a time. Mirrors are more likely to benefit from a monthly clean, especially the bathroom mirror, which often gets sprayed with toothpaste. A little distilled white vinegar buffed with paper towels or newspaper gives a good shine.

Clean cushion covers and throws Keep your chairs and sofas looking good by cleaning the cushion covers and throws regularly.

Clean the oven Keeping a sheet of aluminium foil at the bottom of the oven will help to keep the oven clean by catching any crumbs or spillages and can be changed regularly. If your oven has a lot of grime, you may decide to use a professional oven cleaning product, which can be toxic, so make sure you follow the manufacturer's instructions. For a natural cleaner, sprinkle baking soda on the oven surfaces and rub with a wet steelwool or nylon pad. Then rinse by wiping down with a clean damp cloth.

Dust the areas you normally neglect You will find it much easier to stay on top of cobwebs and the dust that collects on top of curtain rails, blinds, pictures, lights, and lamps if you dust them regularly. Lambswool dusters help to collect dust instead of dispersing it.

Polish wood and brassware When it comes to polishing wood, furniture polish will do, or beeswax for unpolished woods, but make sure you don't put too much on or you could end up with a polish build up. Depending upon use, furniture should be polished once a year. Brass and copper can be cleaned with distilled white vinegar mixed with salt or baking soda, or lemon juice mixed with salt, but do not use on anything plated.

Vacuum the areas you normally neglect It's surprising how much dirt, hair, and crumbs seems to accumulate in places that we rarely see, like under the beds, cupboards, and sofas. Vacuuming these areas regularly helps to keep control of dust mites and textile pests.

Clean the porch or steps outside the front door This makes a huge difference to the first impression of your home. Make sure you sweep up old leaves or dirt first. Then wash down with warm soapy water or a liquid cleanser for difficult stains and dry with an old towel or a cloth.

teamwork

Everyone in the household should get into the habit of cleaning up after themselves. It should be the responsibility of each member of the household to straighten their own room, put their clothes in the hamper, and put their clean clothes away after washing. Just carrying out a few tasks like this will give you a head start.

When it comes to weekly and monthly chores, hold a meeting with everyone who lives in your house and decide how you are going to divide up the tasks between you. Bear in mind the capabilities and available time of each member of the household when delegating. For jobs that are more difficult or boring than others and that no one really wants to do, a rota is probably the answer. Having the agreement of everyone about how the responsibilities are divided is far more likely to lead to a successful workforce.

If you want your home to be a beautiful and functional sanctuary, cleaning is just one of those tasks that you have to get on with, but this doesn't mean that it has to be boring.

Make it fun Keep your spirits up while cleaning by playing your favorite music, a book on tape, or by listening to the radio.

Enlist some help Get your family or roommates to help you. Have a race (but make sure the jobs are done properly). If you have children, turn cleaning into a game and give rewards for tasks well done (but don't expect a perfect job from young children).

Give the right impression If you're short of time, focus only on those areas that guests will see, like the hallway, living room, and bathroom.

Chill out While your intention should be to create a clean and organized home, if cleaning tasks fall by the wayside from time to time, don't let it bother you. Sometimes other things take priority, so go easy on yourself.

get the family to help

If you have a family, encourage them to keep things neat by following these pointers.

Encourage your family to help you save on laundry time by putting their dirty clothes in the right place, proving them with double-compartment clothes hampers, with one section for light clothes and one for dark clothes. Position the hampers in a place where each member usually gets undressed.

To encourage everyone to put their things away, leave a basket at the top and the bottom of the stairs to deposit items that need to be brought up or down stairs. Make it a rule that everyone in the household checks the basket for items before they go up or down stairs empty-handed.

When requesting someone to carry out a task, be specific. For example, instead of asking that your children straighten up the mess in the living room, ask specifically for the toys or the books to be put away—you're much more likely to get the right job done.

Make cleaning up easy. Create easily accessible storage containers like baskets, plastic boxes, trunks, or cupboards to make straightening up a simple task.

the right equipment

One way to make cleaning speedier is to have the right tools ready to use. Keeping a cleaning kit in the kitchen and bathroom will encourage you to use them whenever you need to. For the rest of the house, get yourself a light, open, plastic tool box or bucket. This holds your cleaning essentials and can be carried with you as you go around the house. Also make sure that you can easily access the other tools you need, like the vacuum cleaner, mop, and dustpan and brush. In your bucket you should have dusters, a sponge, rubber gloves, a multipurpose cleaner, and anything else that you feel is especially useful.

A stroll down the cleaning aisle at the supermarket could leave you feeling confused. There are so many choices, each product claiming to do a different job—but are they really necessary? There is no doubt that some cleaning products do their job superbly, but the problem of using manufactured products is that they often contain so many chemicals and can have an unhealthy impact both on people and on the environment. If this is something that concerns you, why not try some of the time-honored natural alternatives, which are easy to come by and simple to use (see opposite).

essential cleaning kit

Dish detergent For dishes, floors, walls, and clothes stains.

Liquid cleanser For grease and grime in the kitchen and bathroom.

A multipurpose surface cleaner For all other surfaces.

Bleach For stained sinks, some kitchen surfaces, and toilets.

Oven cleaner For tackling the inside of your oven.

Furniture polish or beeswax For wooden furniture and banisters.

Window cleaner For cleaning windows.

Rubber gloves For protecting your hands.

Dishcloth Good for wiping down surfaces, but must be washed often.

Sponge with scouring pad Good for getting rid of grime and stains, but should be cleaned thoroughly after use.

Steelwool or nylon pads For some stovetops, ovens, and baking tins.

Dusters and towels For dusting and drying surfaces.

Chamois leather or linen scrim Good for polishing windows and mirrors, although newspaper or paper towels will do.

Old clean toothbrush For cleaning the edges of faucets and stovetops.

Spray bottles For making your cleaning work easier.

Broom, dustpan, and brush Start at the end of the room and sweep the dirt into a pile. Sweep the pile into your dustpan and brush and pour the debris into the rubbish bin.

Vacuum Essential for cleaning carpets and useful for freshening upholstery.

Mop and bucket Useful for washing floors.

the natural selection

Soapflakes Plain soapflakes mixed with hot water and a little washing soda will accomplish most cleaning tasks.

Washing soda crystals Also known as sodium carbonate, washing soda naturally softens the water and cuts through grease and grime with ease. It can be used for cleaning kitchen counters, walls, and hard floors, and is also good for clearing plugholes and drains.

Baking soda Also known as bicarbonate of soda, this is wonderful for most types of cleaning. Mixed with a little water, it is particularly good for cleaning stainless steel and can be used with hot water to soak burnt casserole dishes and pots and pans. As a dry powder it can be sprinkled onto carpets and rugs to soak up odors before vacuuming.

Distilled white vinegar The acid in white vinegar helps to cut through dirt and limescale in an instant. It gives amazing results when used for cleaning glass and tiles, and can also be used for removing tea stains from cups and teapots. When mixed with bicarbonate of soda or salt, it can be used for polishing brass and copper. It is also useful for dealing with pet urine stains.

Lemon juice Lemon juice is not only a great cleaner, but it gives off a wonderfully fresh fragrance, too. It can be used for removing stains and to bleach cutting boards and kitchen counters. When mixed with a little salt, it can also be used for cleaning copper and brass.

Table salt Salt makes an excellent mild disinfectant and can be used as a gentle scouring abrasive.

Essential oils Eucalyptus, grapefruit, lavender, lemon, and pine all make wonderful room disinfectants. Any of these oils can be added to water in a spray bottle to create a lovely, fragrant air freshener (see pages 96–97).

get organized

Once you've cleared your clutter
and given your home a thorough
clean, you should be feeling
good about what you've
achieved. The question is—how
long will it take until your home
is back to the same state it was
in before you started? For most
of us, it's very likely that if we
carry on as usual without
creating a new system to help
us stay in control of our home, it
won't be long before we're back
to square one.

Your ability to stay on top of the clutter and cleaning in your home depends upon having good storage, being choosy about what comes into your home, and having an organized routine.

Creating a routine that becomes second nature is the easiest way to stay on top of your household chores. Your routine needs to be realistic, something that you have time to fit into your lifestyle and are willing to stick with.

The best way to organize your routine is to make a list of the household chores you need to carry out to create the home you desire. Next to each chore, write down how often the chore needs to be done, whether this is every day, every week, or every month. Then, next to each chore, write down how much time you are going to need to complete it. If you're not sure, time yourself next time you do the task. Now go down your list and add up how much time you need to spend on your everyday chores, your weekly chores, and your monthly chores. This will give you a good idea of how much time you need to keep your home looking good.

Think now of how much time you have available each day and each week to devote to your home. If you don't have enough time available to complete all the tasks you've chosen, you may have to lower your aims. You could also consider hiring a cleaner. Either way, you need to bear in mind that if you create a routine that is practical, easily achieved, and takes into consideration your personal quirks, lifestyle, and the sort of people who live in your home, you are far more likely to make your routine a success.

Allocating a schedule for your household chores is only a part of creating a home that runs smoothly—other areas of your life need to be organized, too. The everyday demands on time and energy can create a juggling act for most people. Whether these demands come from jobs, the needs of children, getting the housework done, keeping finances on track, or allowing ourselves time to indulge in a social life, we need to be good time managers if we want our home to function efficiently.

a diary

Procrastination often paralyses people when it comes to organizing their households, especially if they don't know where to begin. So the best place to start is with a diary. When you purchase a diary, make sure you put into it any important dates that you know about. These could be holidays, birthdays, events like parties or weddings, and deadlines like tax returns or car insurance that you know will be coming up.

Look at the month ahead. Are there any events or deadlines that you need to put into your diary for this month? A coffee morning, someone's farewell party, or perhaps bills that need to be paid? If you've worked out your cleaning routine, you can allocate the time you need to get your chores done both weekly and monthly. Now look at the week ahead. Is there anything you need to get done this week?

Using a diary will immediately give you a greater sense of organization. You no longer need to carry dates around in your head and if you refer to your diary every day, you will find it much easier to keep track of everything.

plan your day

Last thing at night or first thing in the morning, put aside at least ten minutes to plan your day ahead. The most effective way to do this is to write a "to do" list. Make sure you put your most important tasks at the top of the list and be realistic. If you really don't have much time, limit yourself and put only about three to five things on your list.

stress-free housekeeping

Be realistic It's no good adopting someone else's housekeeping standards if they don't suit your household and your lifestyle. Be realistic and tailor your schedule to suit you and those you live with.

Make it manageable When faced with a daunting task or a chore you don't have enough time to complete in one go, break it down into sat can be achieved a bit at a time.

Be willing to delegate Partners, roommates, and children are all capable of doing certain tasks, so delegate those that are suitable.

Use your most productive time Recognize when during the day you work most productively and schedule any important activities for this time.

Do the tasks that bring the most rewards When you have a long "to do" list, think about which tasks will make the biggest difference. Doing these tasks first will not only keep you motivated, but will also bring the greatest achievements.

create a household file

Whether you live on your own or with other people, it's a good idea to keep a record of all your household information in one central location. This should include any important numbers and addresses, details of important events, take-out menus, shopping lists, video rental cards, or anything that you or your household use regularly. This information can be kept in a folder, a concertina file or card file, on a bulletin board—whatever you feel is most useful.

If you have a family, you might also want to keep a family diary in the same spot, so that important information, dates, and deadlines are shared.

10 things you can do right now

Clearing and cleaning your home from top to bottom can take time, especially if you have let things slide. Commitment and patience are essential, but the finished result will be worth it. Getting started is the first hurdle, so if you want to make an immediate improvement to your home, try one or more of the following.

1 Choose a clutter hotspot and give away, throw away, or recycle five items. This could be from a pile of paperwork, a shelf overloaded with books, a mantelpiece with too many ornaments, or anywhere that you seem to accumulate items. Letting go is one of the first steps towards purifying your home.

2 Create more space instantly by clearing the floors and counters of anything that shouldn't be there. Take a couple of bags or cardboard boxes and fill them with all the bits and pieces that need sorting out. This helps you gain an immediate feeling of being in control and lets you start cleaning up—but do allocate time to go through each bag or box and sort it out.

3 Add a sparkle to your windows and mirrors. Symbolically, windows represent your view of the world and mirrors represent your view of yourself, so it's not good to leave them dusty and dirty. To get a super clean shine, mix two tablespoons vinegar with one cup of water in a spray mist bottle. Shake and spray onto the windows and mirrors sparingly then wipe off with paper towels or newspaper.

4 Purify your carpets by sprinkling them liberally with salt or baking soda. Leave for a couple of hours before vacuuming. To make vacuuming more pleasant, add a few drops of a cleansing essential oil like lavender, lemon, or orange to the filter of the vacuum cleaner, or place a cotton ball that has been dipped in an essential oil into the vacuum bag.

5 Add new life to white kitchen appliances that have turned yellow. Mix a quarter-cup bleach with two tablespoons baking soda and one and a quarter cups of warm water. Spread on with a sponge and leave for 10 minutes. Rinse off with clean water and dry.

6 Choose a habit that negatively influences your home and change it today. This could be making sure you put things away after you've used them, dealing with your mail as soon as it arrives, or doing the dishes after each meal. Keeping your home clear and clean will only come from adopting good habits, so make these new habits part of your usual routine.

7 Choose something that needs mending—this could be an ornament that needs gluing, a jacket that needs a button, or a toaster that needs repairing. Doing your mending while watching the television or listening to your favorite music will make it less like work. If you need to send something off to be repaired—do it today.

8 Add some hooks to create more space. Look around your home and see whether there are any places where you can add a hook or two. They are great for instantly getting things like keys, aprons, coffee cups, and shopping bags off floors and counters, allowing you to concentrate on purifying the space.

9 Freshen your wardrobe and clothes drawers with sachets of dried lavender, particularly where you have items made of natural fibers like wool, linen, cotton, and silk. This will not only keep your clothes smelling fresh, but also discourage moths.

10 Light some incense. If you don't have time to carry out an incense cleansing ritual (see page 123), choose an incense stick like lemon or pine, which is naturally cleansing, and place it in a holder in the middle of the room while you straighten up and clean. When you've finished in one room, take it with you to the next room and let it burn while you work again.

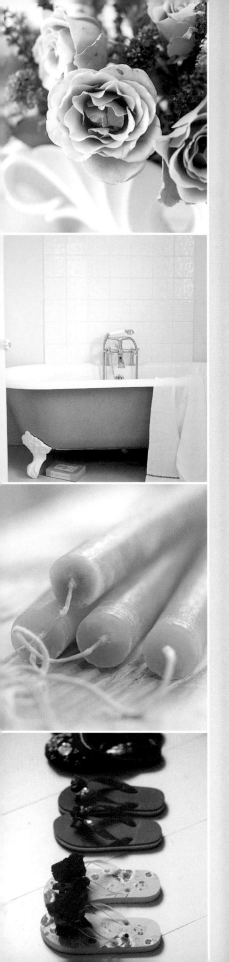

create harmony

add that extra something

By now your home should be clean and tidy, it should be functioning smoothly and at least on the way to having the kind of character that makes you feel good. But that's just the start of creating a home sanctuary. To feel completely at home, you need to add something far more personal and uplifting. You need to create an atmosphere that is uniquely your own.

To turn your home into a sanctuary you need to embrace a feeling of serenity and harmony. Not only will this turn your living environment into somewhere soothing, it will also boost your health and lift your spirits. Clinical studies have demonstrated that views of nature, natural light, harmonious colors, and therapeutic sounds all have the power to enhance our health and feelings of well-being. And there are many other ways to boost our environment, too, such as using crystals, herbs, plants, and beautiful fragrances. Use this chapter as a stimulus to your imagination, and see it as a starting point to pursuing your own ideas. Don't forget to jot down any thoughts in your notebook. You may feel inspired in the most surprising ways, so be sensitive to how you respond to different environments as you transform your home into a sanctuary.

finishing touches

To turn a house into a home you need to evoke feelings
of warmth, comfort, nurture, and protection.

Familiar items These can be any objects that give you a
feeling of security and comfort. For some people this might
be a favorite mug or blanket. For others it could be a well-
loved teddy bear or even a video that conjures up positive
memories. These objects will make you feel as though your
home belongs to you.

Photographs Placing photographs of you, your partner, your
family, and your friends around your home, which conjure up
happy memories, will tap you into those feelings again. It
may also be nice to hang pictures (if you have any) of your
ancestors on your walls or place them on other surfaces to
create a feeling of security and support.

Evocative pictures What sort of scenery inspires you? A
town house? A cottage in the country? A beautiful garden?
Boats on the sea? Think about the sort of buildings, natural
surroundings, and places that make you feel good and
choose drawings, paintings, or photographs that portray these
scenes to hang around your home and inspire positive feelings.

Cushions and soft fabrics Cushions in attractive fabrics are
wonderful for giving your sofas and chairs an inviting feeling.
They help to soften the shape of the furniture, but a few well-
chosen cushions are better than too many, which prevent you
from sitting comfortably. Curtains, sofas, chairs, and throws
made of fabrics that are attractive to touch make a home
more intimate. Velvet, wool, and cotton are particularly nice to
feel and, when combined with warm colors or patterns, give
an instant glow to a room.

Rugs A few well-chosen rugs will warm up wooden or tiled
floors and add a splash of color to carpeting. If you plan to sit
on your rug or have children who would like to play on it,
make sure you opt for something soft and welcoming rather
than hard-wearing materials such as sisal and jute.

Plants and flowers Having a plant or vase of flowers in a
room adds a feeling that your home is being nurtured and
appreciated. Flowering plants or flowers are particularly nice if
you want to add color and warmth to a room.

Table lamps Table lamps are one of the fastest ways, next to candles, to create a cosy atmosphere. One or two table lamps in the living room will produce a soothing, relaxing light. Choose lampshades with slight yellow, orange, or pink tones to create a warming glow.

An open fire An open fire is unequalled when it comes to conjuring up a feeling of warmth and intimacy. In ancient times, the hearth was regarded as a magical place, somewhere that provided heat and nourishment. Nowadays, gas open fires have made the hearth more convenient, since they can be automatically lit and don't require cleaning out. If an open fire is not practical for you, candles—although a lot smaller—can create the same atmosphere.

find your colors

Changing the color of your walls, floors, or furnishings is one of the quickest ways to alter the environment in which you live. When we begin to appreciate the far-reaching effects of color on ourselves and those around us, we can incorporate the colors that suit us best into our home. This will not only cut down on the stress we experience, but enhance our confidence and well-being, too.

We each experience color in a very personal way and, while some colors create a feeling of harmony, others drain our energy. Changing the colors around you can have a dramatic effect so before you do anything drastic, experiment with swatches of color and paint samples. Refer to the style boards that you made earlier and any notes you've made about color in your notebook. Remember that colors can also look quite different in the store from how they look when you get them home. This is to do with light and also with how colors work together. For example, a rich red carpet may look delightfully vibrant in the shop but when you get it home and place it next to something orange, it may just clash. Think about the purpose of each room and how colors complement each other as you devise your color scheme.

Warm and cool colors Colors can be divided into warm and cool, depending upon the visual warmth they give off. Warm colors—essentially those colors based on red and orange—tend to advance visually, which means they appear to come closer. Warm colors

should be used in rooms that feel or appear cold, are large, or don't receive much sunlight. Cool colors, on the other hand, are based on blue and are described as receding because they give a feeling of distance. They are useful for decorating small rooms or rooms that feel too hot or sunny. Cool colors can be warmed by the addition of a small amount of red, while warm colors can be cooled by the addition of a small amount of blue. Generally, the warm colors like red, orange, and yellow are best used in areas in your home where there is lots of activity like kitchens, playrooms, or recreation areas. The cool colors, which help us relax or think, are best suited for bedrooms, bathrooms, and home offices.

Light and dark colors Light colors make a room look larger and lighter, while dark colors reduce the amount of light reflected. If you have a large room, a high ceiling, or want to create more intimacy, opt for darker, warmer colors. If you have a small room or a room that receives little natural light, opt for lighter, brighter colors to give the illusion of more space and light.

Neutral colors Neutral colors such as cream, beige, gray, and white or off-white are also good for expanding smaller rooms and bringing in light. They are equally excellent for providing a neutral background for colorful pictures and furnishings. Depending upon the undertone, a neutral color can be either warm or cool. For example, white mixed with a little blue will be cool, while white mixed with a little red, to give it a pink tint, will be warm.

color codes

Colors have the power to make us feel happy or sad, calm or excited, and each color has an influence and symbolism of its own.

Red is invigorating with its associations of warmth, daring, and passion. It's linked with carnal love and intimacy, the hearth, fire, and action.

Purple is the color of royalty and also of mysticism. It is good for encouraging psychic ability and spiritual guidance.

Blue is restful, encourages serenity, and helps meditation. It's one of the healing colors, and deep blue is associated with good communications.

Yellow is vivid and cheerful, the color of hope. It's also associated with mental work and helps to lift the mood.

Green is calming and balancing, symbolizing nature and healing. In yogic teaching, love is associated with green and pink. Green has been found to help concentration and calm nerves.

Orange is vivid, sociable, and exciting. It's believed to stimulate the appetite and is associated with creativity.

Brown is warm, natural, and robust, symbolizing the earth.

Black is a dramatic, mysterious, and protecting color, conveying a sense of the unknown. Too much black can be negative but a small amount is grounding.

White conveys light and purity. It provides an uncomplicated background for other colors and patterns, but can also appear clinical and austere.

lovely lighting

When thinking about lighting for a particular room you must first analyse the function of the room and then decide what is required. Most rooms need an acceptable level of general lighting, which can be provided by a central pendant or chandelier, and controlled by dimmer switches, allowing you to alter the level of illumination. Areas where you work or relax, however, will need something extra. There are three distinct types of lighting in the home—general, task, and specific lighting. The type of lighting you choose will depend upon what you want the lighting to achieve and the type of atmosphere you would like to create.

- General lighting delivers light throughout a room and does not concentrate on any particular area. This can be in the form of central pendants, downlighters, uplighters (which bounce reflected light from the ceiling), floor lamps, or table lamps.
- Task lighting provides a suitable light for tasks such as reading, writing, and sewing. Task lighting is required when the level of general lighting is inadequate and more local light is needed. Examples of task lights are reading lights and the light in the hood of the stove.
- Specific lighting highlights special features in a room without allowing too much light to spill over into areas where it is not wanted. All spotlights fall into this category because they project a tightly controlled beam of bright light.

colored lights

When you are investing in lampshades for your home, remember that colored light is said to have a therapeutic effect. You may even want to invest in tinted lightbulbs.

Blue light is soothing and cooling. Use it to cool hot rooms or to calm yourself when you are feeling angry.

Green light is good for relaxing, unwinding, and balancing the emotions.

Orange light is warming and stimulating; it helps to lift the mood and combat depression.

Pink light encourages a warm, loving, and nurturing environment.

Red light creates a warming, exotic, and emotionally arousing atmosphere.

Violet light calms and lifts the spirit, helps to harmonize your mental and emotional state.

bring light into your home

No form of artificial lighting can match the beauty of sunlight, so try to allow as much natural light into your home as possible. Here are some ways to bring more light into your home:

• Keep your windows clean.

• Keep your windows free from obstructions.

• Draw curtains back as far as possible and keep blinds up during the day.

• Opt for curtains or blinds that are lighter in color so that they don't absorb the light.

• If you have lace curtains, consider opting for café-style ones that cover only half of the window.

• Open your windows frequently to let the light into your home.

• Hang mirrors where they can reflect natural light from windows.

• Consider installing full-spectrum lighting if you feel that you are suffering from a lack of light.

• Paint your walls a light color and choose lighter, brighter fabrics for your furnishings.

the air you breathe

Air is the primary source of our life energy, so it is important to pay attention to the quality of the air in our homes. For many of us, indoor pollution can be a serious health concern, especially since most of us now spend so much time indoors. We are surrounded by man-made substances and materials, all of which can create a build-up of toxins in our environment. There are many ways to improve the quality of air in your home, most of which are inexpensive. Below are a few suggestions:

- Decorate and furnish your home with as many natural materials as possible.
- Make your household a no-smoking zone.
- Open doors and windows to encourage fresh air to circulate.
- Hang dry-cleaned garments outside to let them air before hanging them in the closet.
- Cut down on the amount of plastic you use in your home.
- Limit your use of chemical household products.
- Use an aromatherapy burner with an essential oil like eucalyptus or lavender to scent and disinfect the air naturally.

Some people are more sensitive to polluted environments than others and as a consequence, suffer from physical ailments like allergies, headaches, and asthma. For many people, plants help to alleviate this, not only because they absorb toxins and give out oxygen, but also because many plants emit moisture, which counteracts the dryness caused by indoor heating and air conditioning. Plants also have a symbolism of their own, which is used by feng shui practitioners today (see opposite).

detox plants

These plants are especially good for improving air quality:

Aloe vera *(Aloe barbadensis)*

Bamboo palm *(Chamaedorea seifrizii)*

English ivy *(Hedera helix)*

Peace lily *(Spathiphyllum)*

Rubber plant *(Ficus robusta)*

Spider plant *(Chlorophytum comosum)*

Boston fern *(Nephrolepis bostoniensis)*

Chinese evergreen *(Aglaonema crispum)*

Chrysanthemum *(Chrysanthemum morifolium)*

Dracaena *(Dracaena deremensis)*

plant symbolism

Feng shui practitioners believe that plants can be used to increase the "chi" or energy in the home, bringing more luck into the environment.

Wax begonia *(Begonia semperflorens)*: Stability.

Boston fern *(Nephrolepis bostoniensis)*: Vitality.

Cyclamen *(Cyclamen persicum)*: Interest.

Ivy *(Hedera helix)*: Loyalty.

Money plant *(Crassula ovata)*: Money.

Peace lily *(Spathiphyllum)*: Peace.

Poinsettia *(Euphorbia pulcherrima)*: Glory.

Spider plant *(Chlorophytum comosum)*: Variety.

herbal magic

In days gone by, herbs were an essential part of every household. As well as being used for flavoring and preserving food and for making medicine for both people and animals, herbs were also used for keeping pests at bay and for purifying and adding fragrance to the air inside the home.

In fact, before the days of carpets and other permanent floorcoverings, dried herbs were often spread over the floor to absorb dirt and give off a pleasant fragrance when stepped on. Some herbs such as lavender, catmint, and tansy also had medicinal properties and were used in helping prevent pest infestations, deterring unwanted guests like fleas and rats. When the herbs were no longer fresh, they were simply swept up and replaced with fresh ones. These were known as "strewing herbs."

Placing herb-filled sachets, such as lavender bags, in closets or drawers was also done, not just to perfume clothes and linens but also to keep moths at bay. Herbs like lavender and rue were burnt as air cleansers, too, to purify and freshen the air, particularly after someone had been ill. In a similar way, herbs, leaves, petals, and flower buds were used in scented mixtures known as potpourri. The name potpourri, literally translates from French as "rotted pot" because the original method of making potpourri was to place semi-dried herbs with salt in a bowl, causing them to give off their fragrance by fermenting. Nowadays, most pot pourri is made by a dry method, which is easier to create and more attractive to look at.

Herbs are still as useful today as they were centuries ago. They can provide a healthier alternative to many manufactured household products and can still be used in a variety of different ways around the home. One way to combine both the sensual and practical uses of herbs is to make an herb cushion filled with dried hops to use as an aid for sleeping. The weight and warmth of your head will release the fragrance of the herbs, helping dissolve feelings of stress and tension.

uplifting herb potpourri

2 cups (450 ml) dried lemon peel
2 cups (450 ml) dried orange peel
2 cups (450 ml) dried rose petals
1 cup (225 ml) dried basil leaves
1 cup (225 ml) dried lavender flowers
2 drops grapefruit essential oil
2 drops geranium essential oil
2 drops orange essential oil

Mix the above ingredients together and display the potpourri in an attractive bowl or container that allows the scent to escape. Stir the contents every now and again to release the scent. Potpourri should remain fragrant for several months, although both the color and scent will gradually fade. You can refresh the mixture by adding a few more drops of essential oil when the fragrance has faded.

herbs and their protective properties

Aloe vera Guards against negative influences and prevents household accidents.

Camomile Scatter around the house boundary to protect property.

Dill Tie with red thread and hang from the ceiling next to the front door to keep away harmful predators.

Fennel Hang in windows to deter any unwanted visitors.

Rosemary Burn as incense, hang it around the house, or place in potpourri to repel thieves.

scent sense

You may not realize it, but your house has a particular aroma. To you it just smells like home, to guests, the aroma of your house communicates a powerful—and often subconscious—message about the kind of person you are. Our sense of smell is closely connected to our feelings, our memory, and our psychological well-being.

We tend to block out unpleasant odors in our own homes. We find we can ignore that slight odor of carpet underlay or the smell of wet dog that hangs around the hall closet. But bad smells insidiously create a gloomy atmosphere. Go around your house and take some deep sniffs. Does it smell good? Are you secretly proud of the delicious aroma of your home? Or slightly ashamed? Letting unwanted scents take over your home is letting the side down.

By now, you should have cleaned your home from top to bottom and it should smell of furniture polish and fresh air, so it's time to introduce some new, delicious scents. Think of some aromas that you love and see whether you can introduce any of these into your home right away. Think of percolating coffee, a bouquet of roses, freshly baked bread, or cut grass.

If you want to achieve a specific emotional reaction like a feeling of tranquillity or joy, try using essential oils. Each oil has its own unique fragrance, which is said to subtly influence your brainwave patterns and alter your feelings and the atmosphere of your home. You may need to experiment to find the right fragrance or the right mixture of fragrances to suit your home or your mood. Some fragrances will soothe and relax, while others will lift your spirits or even act as an aphrodisiac. Some essential oils also have natural disinfecting properties, so offer the added bonus of cleaning the atmosphere as well as altering the ambience. Use a diffuser or a ceramic ring that fits on a lightbulb—or try making your own air freshener. All you need is a mist spray bottle, then add 25 drops of essential oil to two tablespoons of water and shake before spraying.

essential oils for lifting the atmosphere	
Bergamot	Healing and cleansing. Good for balancing the atmosphere and the emotions.
Camomile	Soothing, calming, and healing. Good for balancing the atmosphere and the emotions.
Clove	Good room disinfectant. Helps to stimulate and warm the atmosphere.
Eucalyptus	Good room disinfectant. Helps with clear thinking and soothes heated emotions.
Frankincense	Helps with psychic cleansing and purifying, enhances meditation and soothes grief.
Geranium	Helps to boost self-esteem. Soothes fear, discontentment, and heartache.
Grapefruit	Good room disinfectant. Helps to relieve self-doubt, dependency, frustration, and grief.
Jasmine	Helps to lift depression and create a more joyful atmosphere.
Lavender	Good room disinfectant. Healing and balancing. Helps with fears, trauma, worry, and burnout.
Lemon	Good room disinfectant. Helps with mental clarity and optimism.
Neroli	Helps to lift depression and create a more joyful atmosphere. Energizes and protects the emotions.
Orange	Helps with worry, burnout, lethargy, depression, and emotional balance.
Pine	Good room disinfectant. Helps with transforming regrets, self-blame, and feelings of inadequacy.
Rose	Aphrodisiac. Lifting and harmonizing. Helps to heal a broken heart and create strong boundaries.
Rosemary	Purifying and stimulating. Helps to attract positive energies and mental clarity.
Vetiver	Good for balancing, energizing, grounding, and stabilizing the atmosphere.
Ylang Ylang	Aphrodisiac. Helps with relaxing, releasing anger, anxiety, and irritability.

Important: Essential oils are potent and should never be applied directly to the skin or put anywhere near the eyes.

sweet sounds

As with all the senses, some people are more sensitive to sounds than others, but if you want to create a home that acts like a sanctuary, having peace and quiet or harmonious sounds around you is important. Sounds such as traffic noise, slamming doors, and certain types of music can produce a variety of stress-related responses —including raised blood pressure and increased heart rate.

Music has been recognized as an essential part of healing, meditation, and religious experience in many cultures. Most people have listened to their favorite music at one time or another and felt an instant change of mood. In Eastern traditions sacred sounds like chants were used in healing rituals and to enhance spiritual awareness. Shamans have long used music combined with chants and rhythmic movement to induce an altered state of consciousness. The ancient Chinese believed that music was the basis of all things and Confucius suggested that if the music of a kingdom changed, then the attitude of its people would change,

too. For the Ancient Greeks the healing power of music was applied to help digestion, aid sleep, and treat mental problems. Plato, Aristotle, and Pythagoras all had a keen interest in music and offered many ideas on music in healing, education, and culture.

Studies have shown that music affects the pulse rate, skin temperature, blood pressure, muscle tension, and brainwave activity. It can help alleviate pain, speed post-operative recovery, and bring temporary relief to people suffering from debilitating illnesses. But the wrong type of music can also have harmful effects, encouraging aggression and a sense of unease. If you share your home with others whose musical taste conflicts, investing in a set of headphones could well change your life.

It's impossible to generalize too much about the effects of different kinds of music, but in general, pop music, rock and roll, gospel, and Latino tend to lift the spirits and speed

everything up. Classical music calms things down and creates a sense of harmony. New Age music is said to expand consciousness and encourage a feeling of well-being, as does chanting. Another way to create a sense of harmony and balance in your home is to listen to the sounds of nature—either by having something like a water fountain nearby or by playing nature sounds on the stereo. Waves lapping on the seashore, flowing streams, or bird song can help to lower blood pressure and pulse rate, reduce anxiety levels and promote a feeling of calmness and well-being—choose whatever feels good to you.

Total silence will sometimes help you to relax, concentrate, and sleep, but if you live in an urban area it may be difficult to get rid of background noise. If this is a problem for you, look at ways of cutting down incoming noise. Double-glazed or storm windows may do the trick.

Finally, think about the noise you create. Do you have the TV or the radio on all the time? Do you shout from room to room? Allowing silence into your home can be a little bit scary because it forces you to listen to what's going on inside your own mind. But that listening is one of the first steps to achieving tranquillity.

crystal energy

Precious and semi-precious stones have long been valued for their beauty and supposed healing properties. Like many alternative therapies, the true power of crystals still remains unknown, however it is believed that crystals can be used to rebalance energy in the home. Heating, electrical appliances, and man-made furnishings are all said to generate negative energy, which can be neutralized by crystals. However, too many crystals in the home can have an overpowering effect that may make the occupants feel uncomfortable, so it's important to experiment.

There are no rules as to where to place crystals, but here are some suggestions:

• An obsidian sphere or an amethyst facing or near the doors in your home will enhance the feeling of protection.

• A rose quartz opposite the front door to greet visitors will feel welcoming.

• A rose quartz and amethyst in the center or to one side of the room will encourage a positive environment.

• A clear quartz or citrine in the area where you work or study will enhance concentration.

• To absorb the energy of electrical equipment like computers and televisions, place a large amethyst, obsidian or unakite, or a bowl of smaller stones, near the equipment.

• Arrange a bowl of smaller citrines or one large citrine by the telephone to enhance your conversations.

• A clear quartz, a fluorite, or a malachite in the room in which you choose to meditate will enhance the energy around you.

• Place three small amethysts or rose quartz under your bed—one under the top center of the bed, the other two under each corner at the foot of the bed. Some people find that large crystals in the bedroom can disturb their sleep so see what suits you best.

cleanse your crystal

When you bring a new crystal home the first thing you need to do is cleanse it of negative energy. There are a number of ways to do this:

Running water Place your crystal under the cold water faucet to cleanse away old energy. You can also place your crystal in a bowl of water containing sea salt for a couple of hours, but make sure that the crystal is not water soluble or easily scratched.

Sunlight Revitalize your crystal by placing it outside in the sun for a day. You can also do this after you have cleansed your crystal in running water.

Sound You can purify your crystal by placing it near beautiful music or ringing a bell with a clear tone next to it.

crystal sensitivity		
Many crystals are sensitive to light, heat, or water, which means that they may fracture, dissolve, or lose their color if cleansed in the wrong way.		
Water-sensitive crystals	Halite, selenite, lapis lazuli, malachite, turquoise.	
Light-sensitive crystals	Amethyst, rose quartz, turquoise.	
Heat-sensitive crystals	Amethyst, quartz, lapis lazuli, malachite, tourmaline, turquoise.	
Scratch-sensitive crystals	Metallic crystals, celestite, malachite, rhodochrosite, fluorite, apatite, lapis lazuli, sodalite, turquoise, hematite, moonstone.	

common crystals and their properties	
Agate	Calms, stabilizes, and helps with challenges.
Amethyst	Cleanses, protects, absorbs atmospheric pollution, and aids sleep.
Aquamarine	Reduces fear and stress, encourages creativity, protects against pollutants.
Aventurine quartz	Promotes overall well-being, enhances creativity, and soothes stress.
Bloodstone	Purifies, strengthens, and improves decision-making.
Celestite	Revitalizes, regenerates, and helps dream recall.
Citrine	Dispels fear, encourages openness and positivity, and helps with absorbing information.
Clear quartz	Helps with balance, purity, concentration, and meditation.
Fluorite	Protects, energizes, calms, and is good for meditation.
Hematite	Protects, grounds, and helps to transform negativity.
Jade	Encourages harmony, prolongs life, protects, and aids dreams and sleep.
Lapis lazuli	Helps with mental clarity, protects against depression, and boosts the immune system.
Moonstone	Calms and balances the emotions and helps with intuition.
Malachite	Lifts the spirits, calms and harmonizes the environment, good for meditation.
Obsidian	Adds strength and protection and absorbs negative influences.
Rose quartz	Encourages a loving and peaceful atmosphere and heightens self-esteem.
Sodalite	Creates harmony, increases spiritual awareness, and aids sleep.
Turquoise	Helps with communication, encourages self-awareness.
Tiger's eye	Helps with inner strength, optimism, and challenges.
Unakite	Calms the environment and negates the effects of electromagnetic pollution.

your spiritual home

Your home should be a place
that refreshes the soul and
revives the spirit. Within your
sanctuary you can create a still,
calm space where you can
center yourself and listen to your
own inner voice, and where you
can remind yourself of just what
it means to be you.

One of the most important elements in creating a home is making it a welcoming space where you feel a sense of belonging. The fastest way to do this is to add those things that are familiar to you, that give you a sense of reassurance and security, whether these are childhood toys, photographs, or a favorite chair. Also important is incorporating a feeling of your family, your history, or your culture—all these things will help you feel as though your space belongs to you.

But as well as connecting to your own roots, your home should let you express yourself as a spiritual being. If you are religious, you may want to display icons or religious artefacts or create a place for prayer. If your spiritual instincts are more eclectic, you will probably choose to express yourself in other ways. By letting your creativity, flourish you are connecting with your spirit, which is a deeply personal act. This could be as simple as arranging a vase of flowers or a bowl of stones, or as profound as playing a beloved musical instrument or meditating. According to Zen Buddhist teaching, it is the intention with which we do things that is important.

an altar

Your home should be a place that not only provides a safe refuge from the outside world, but also encourages and inspires you to be all that you can be. For this reason you should have in your home reminders of the symbols, images, and objects that connect you to the people, situations, and qualities in your life that are important to you.

One way of doing this is to create an altar in your home where you can display the treasures that tune you into positive and harmonious feelings. This should be a part of your home that acts as a manifestation area, a focus point, or a dream space where you enjoy, attract, and celebrate those things that are most important to you. There is no need to build an altar specially—a mantelpiece, dressing table, window sill, or shelf will do, or you can choose more than one spot to place your precious symbols and artefacts. Just make sure the location you choose is somewhere that makes you feel calm, and somewhere that you see often, so that you are reminded and uplifted by your positive treasures throughout the day.

The purpose of an altar is to help you get in touch with your positive feelings and your potential. Whatever you place on your altar should have a meaningful

association for you and be pleasing to look at. Some of the items should act as "power tools" or symbols, which help you to affirm and attract those qualities and situations into your life that you desire, for example a picture of someone who has qualities you admire or a symbol that represents a goal you are working on. Of course the objects and symbols you place on your altar will change and evolve over time as you develop and grow, and only you can determine what works for you, but below are some suggestions:

- Photographs of family, friends, pets, or special places
- Religious/spiritual images
- Crystals
- Fresh flowers or plants
- Written words that have a special meaning for you
- Symbols that have a meaning for you (see pages 108–109)
- Objects that have special significance
- Potpourri or an essential oil burner that creates an attractive fragrance

a treasure box

You may find an altar unappealing or you may want to keep some of your most precious objects private. If so, why not make yourself a treasure box. Any box will do—a shoe box is ideal. You can place inside your box anything that is important to you, be it pictures or objects. If you want to make your box look a little more special, you could cover it in pictures that are important to you or in attractive wrapping paper.

the power of symbols

Whether we realize it or not, most of our homes are full of symbols that relate to who we are, what we want, and what we believe in. Symbolism has been used for millennia to communicate desires and intentions, to inspire collective action, and bring people together. All around the world, from the totems of the Native Americans, to the hieroglyphics of the Egyptians and the religious icons of the Greek Orthodox church, symbolism has played a large part in our sense of belonging and our feeling of purpose in the world. Even today people pray and fight under emblems and banners that have symbolic significance to them, and use symbols to tune themselves into particular qualities and feelings.

A symbol can be anything: an object, a person, an image, a color, a number—anything that holds a meaning beyond itself.

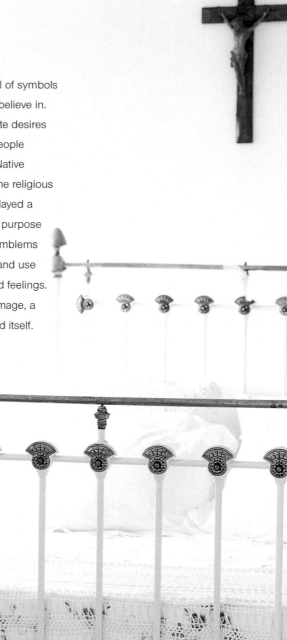

For example the Chinese symbol of yin and yang represents the complementary forces of life—positive and negative and male and female—while the crucifix represents eternal life, faith, forgiveness, and redemption.

It may be that symbols hold their power not only because of their historic connotations, but also because we respond to them almost instinctively. In more recent times, the symbols we have adopted have often been connected to our lifestyle, our aspirations, and our goals.

Symbols can inspire us to adopt particular qualities, feelings, and actions and can be wonderful tools to have around us to encourage a positive and harmonious living environment. Although certain symbols have specific meanings, how you relate to a symbol is personal to you and you should choose a symbolic object or image based on your own instincts.

When it comes to our homes there are many symbols that can encourage the kinds of feelings and qualities we need in order to create a positive atmosphere around us. Below are some of the best-known symbols:

balance and harmony

The scales Balance, equality, and justice.
The harp Spiritual harmony.
The color green Balancing and soothing.
Yin and yang symbol Balance and equality.
Buddha Balance, joy, and spiritual growth.

peace and tranquillity

Calm water Calm emotions, purity, and tranquillity.
The color blue Calming and tranquil.
Blue sky Tranquillity and freedom.
A dove Peace.

healing

Archangel Raphael Physical and emotional healing.
Archangel Uriel Wisdom, healing, and recovery.
An apple Youth, health, and healing.
The snake Potency and strength.

protection

Archangel Michael Overcoming obstacles, protection, wisdom.
The lion Courage and protection.
The dragon Strength, endurance, and power.
A sword Protection.

uplifting atmosphere

Archangel Gabriel Truth, hope, and purpose.
The sun Warmth and positivity.
The color yellow Positivity, lifts the spirits.
A rainbow Luck and spiritual guidance.
A star Hope and good fortune.

honor your history

Part of creating an atmosphere of security and stability in your home is honoring who you really are. Although you are creating yourself from moment to moment, you also have a history and a powerful pathway that you have followed to become who you are now.

Honoring your past puts you in touch with the greater wheel of life and your importance in the chain of history. Even people who dislike much of their past can find times that created a feeling of joy or success. To bring these feelings into your home, find something that symbolizes the positive times, such as a photograph or a toy, and place it somewhere special—perhaps on a mantelpiece, a dressing table, or a special shelf—where you will be reminded of those happy times.

Many cultures and religions around the world still celebrate and revere their connection to their ancestors. The Celts viewed ancestral worship as a continuation of the Celtic spirit and believed their ancestors were watching over them and would strengthen the Tribal Soul. Some Chinese believed that the successes of the previous generations could be aligned with their own energy and added to their own successes, and in some forms of feng shui, there is still a part of the home that is put aside to pay homage to the elders and ancestors.

Another way to bring a sense of history into your home is by honoring the power of myths, legends, and traditions. Mythical or legendary tales and characters can hold a symbolic feeling of belonging for some people, particularly if those myths or legends come from your culture.

five ways to bring your history into your home

1 Lay out your family tree.

2 Research the meaning of your family name or something
  that represents your family, like a tartan or a coat of arms.

3 Display photographs of you as a child and of those you love.

4 Display inherited possessions.

5 Display symbols that represent your culture or a family tradition.

space clearing

Our homes are our sacred space, a place where we should feel safe and comfortable, where we can shut out the world and feel free to be ourselves. However, the tension and stresses that we endure in our day-to-day lives can build up, leaving a negative impression on the atmosphere of our homes.

The best way to combat this tense atmosphere and turn your home back into your sanctuary is to carry out a space clearing ritual (see opposite). Most houses could do with a space clearing ritual to refresh the atmosphere, particularly if you've had an argument, if someone has been ill, or if you are having trouble sleeping.

efficient space clearing

1 Carry out the space clearing ritual after you have straightened up and cleaned your home.

2 Carry out the ritual during the day between the time of a New and Full Moon.

3 Make sure that you are in a positive frame of mind when you carry out the ritual.

4 Try to put aside time to do your ritual when you won't be interrupted.

5 If you feel the atmosphere in your home is particularly muggy, use more salt in the ritual (see opposite).

space clearing ritual

You will need:

A bowl of salt
A bowl of water
A lavender incense stick
A long white candle

1 Open all the doors and windows in the house.

2 Gather together your equipment and bless the salt, water, incense stick, and candle with your good intentions, stating that you would like them to help you clear and renew the energy of your home.

3 Starting at the front door, hold your bowl of salt and walk around the house in a clockwise pattern. Also follow a clockwise direction within each room. Sprinkle the salt with your dominant hand (the hand that you write with) as you slowly walk through the house. As you do this, imagine the salt neutralizing any negative energy in the house. Say out loud or to yourself: "May this salt of the earth absorb all negative and unwanted energies from this place and replace them with love, peace and joy for everyone who lives in this home." Go through the whole house until you have covered all the areas.

4 Go back to the front door. This time walk slowly through the house in a clockwise direction with your lighted candle, saying: "May this candle of fire burn up all negative and unwanted energies from this place and replace them with love, peace, and joy for everyone who lives in this home."

5 Start again at the front door, this time with the lighted lavender incense stick. Go through the house again as before, this time stating: "May this joss incense of air dissolve all negative and unwanted energies from this place and replace them with love, peace, and joy for everyone who lives in this home." Extinguish your incense stick and go back to the front door.

6 Finally, take your bowl of water and walk slowly around your home in a clockwise direction, sprinkling water as you go and saying: "May this water purify all negative and unwanted energies from this place and replace them with love, peace, and joy for everyone who lives in this home."

7 Finish the ritual by giving thanks to the elements for cleaning your house.

year-round purity

keep up the momentum

If you've worked through the book; decided what you want to achieve, cleared your clutter, given your home a good clean, set yourself a workable routine, and added those finishing touches that make your home into a place that you love—give yourself a pat on the back!

Creating the perfect place to live is a dynamic process and takes time, energy, and dedication. Adopting new habits and changing routines takes persistence and it's easy to fall back into old ways, to get swept up with current distractions, or just lose your drive. If you live a busy life, have a demanding career, children, or both, there are bound to be times when your harmonious home reverts to chaos—so take this in your stride. With a little patience and hard work you'll have your home sanctuary back in no time.

However, if you find yourself constantly unable to cope, feeling tired or overstretched just trying to keep up, then you need to look at where your life is not in balance. Being out of balance will ultimately result in feeling stressed and stress doesn't just make us ill by undermining our natural defenses, it also encourages unhealthy behavior and unhappiness. For example, when we're tired we often drink too much caffeine to get us going and then drink too much alcohol to unwind. We graze on convenience food instead of feeding ourselves nutritious meals and flop in front of the television like a couch potato in an attempt to relax. Our quality of life goes out of the window and this has a negative influence on ourselves, our relationships, and our home.

Of course some stress is essential to keep us feeling motivated and interested in life, but if you're feeling overly challenged and tired, trying to keep up with a schedule that really doesn't seem to be working, then you need to step back and see what needs to be changed. Being happy is far more important than trying to achieve a perfect home, so don't punish yourself if you don't manage to stay on top of everything all the time. Find your own balance and settle for what best suits you and those you live with.

find your own balance

We all have our own personal sense of balance. For some of us this means being active most of the time, for others it means having plenty of time to sit, think, and relax. If you're a morning person, you'll prefer to do most of your hard work before lunch, but if you're a night owl you might not get going until the evening. Whatever your body's natural rhythm, if you try to work with it, you'll find your own sense of balance much easier to achieve.

Not so long ago people's lives were dictated by the phases of the Moon and the changing of the seasons, but with the advent of developments like electric lighting and indoor heating, the rhythm of our lives has become more and more artificial. Although we often forget that we are part of nature, our bodies still have their own natural body clock, which is affected by the Moon, the Sun, and the seasons.

If you are having trouble finding a sense of balance, it may be worth looking at ways you can work with these natural rhythms. Reminding yourself of the season by bringing the natural world into your home is a great way of staying grounded, as is keeping in touch with the cycles of the Moon. Most people know about the Moon's powerful influence over the tides of the earth and since the physical body is mainly composed of water, it is not illogical to conclude that the waxing and waning of the Moon is likely to affect human beings too.

It has long been believed that the Moon has a powerful influence over all living things. Gardeners still plant and reap by the Moon's phases and, until recently, Moon madness or lunacy—which comes from the Latin word Luna meaning Moon—was taken seriously.

The Moon's cycle is roughly 29 and a half days and begins at the New Moon, which is usually invisible. The Moon then gradually waxes (gets bigger) until it becomes a Full Moon. After this point, the Moon wanes (gets smaller) until it becomes an invisible New Moon again. When it comes to using the rhythms of the Moon to improve your life or your home, the phases below are a useful guideline:

New Moon This is the best time to start something new, like a new habit or routine.

Waxing Moon This is the time for doing anything that you would like to increase in size or would like to give extra energy to.

Full Moon This is an excellent time to find a solution to a problem or protect or purify your home.

Waning Moon Now is the time to give up bad habits, clear out your clutter, and rest.

the great spring clean

Of all the Pagan festivals, Imbolc, the celebration of spring (also known as Groundhog Day) is probably the most important when it comes to our homes. Imbolc, which takes place at the beginning of February, was always celebrated as the time for spring cleaning. Later, the grease and grime left by the use of oil, gas, and candles for heating and lighting made spring cleaning even more essential. Sometimes winter curtains and covers would be changed for something more summery. The winter furnishings would be cleaned thoroughly and put away until autumn, when another big house clean took place.

The best way to get your spring cleaning done is to make a list of all the jobs you want to do, set aside a long weekend, or a week, and make a commitment to keep going until the tasks are done. The whole point of a spring or autumn clean is to scrub those furnishings and areas in your home that don't usually get done during the year. In your home notebook, you should keep a record of what you need to do for each big clean and, gradually, you will evolve your own list of spring cleaning jobs.

There are some tasks listed opposite that you will probably need to do, but your own home will have some unique features, for example floors that need waxing or a large Aga stove to clean and service. Before you start, make sure you have all your equipment at hand.

Clear the ceilings of cobwebs and wash down the walls You need to start at the top so that you can vacuum afterwards anything that falls to the floor. Pollution, cigarette smoke, fingerprints, and daily bumps and scrapes often leave stains and marks on the walls. Don't forget to wash behind pictures and mirrors and dust the tops of frames.

Clean and straighten up your cupboards, closets, and drawers Take everything out of your cupboards, closets, and drawers and give things a thorough clean before putting them back. This is a major job, so do it one cupboard at a time. Kitchen cupboards should really get this treatment at least twice a year; this is a good time to throw out any out-of-date food.

Clean rugs and mats Take rugs and mats outside and beat them with a carpet broom or a normal broom to get the dust out. Handmade carpets benefit from some time airing in the sun. You may want to have them cleaned professionally.

Shampoo your carpets This makes a world of difference to the freshness of your home. You may want to hire a machine to do this effectively.

Clean under your furniture and appliances Clean and vacuum under any furniture that you don't usually manage to get to, like beds, chests of drawers, and sofas.

Clean pillows, comforters, and pillows If you can't fit these into your washing machine, take them to the laundromat where they have much larger machines.

Air mattresses Stand them up, beat them, and if possible put them in the sun.

Clean your curtains If you have the storage space and the money, you can put up summer curtains and swap them back to your winter curtains in autumn.

spiritual spring clean

Certain places fill us with a feeling of peace and tranquillity. We feel good just being there. That is what you want your home to feel like. You've cleaned it, maybe you've redecorated, you've thrown away your clutter and displayed a few choice pieces to perfection—but still something isn't quite right. It's time to try some spiritual purification.

Walk around your home to see whether there are any particular areas that feel uncomfortable to you. It's hard to be precise about what constitutes a "bad atmosphere," but it's likely to give you a feeling of being cold, tense, or generally unhappy. When you come across feelings like this in your home, you may find that all you need to do is add warmer, lighter colors to the décor, open the windows, or change the lighting. But if an uncomfortable atmosphere persists, cleansing the air with incense could be the answer. This is a particularly good technique to use if you think the atmosphere has been caused by tension between people, an unhappy event, or an area of your home that has gone unloved. Whatever the cause of a bad feeling in any part of your home, it's essential that you deal with it so concentrate on any specific trouble spots first and then continue with a general atmospheric clean.

Cleansing the atmosphere with incense is one of the fastest ways to clear the energy in your home. The practice dates back thousands of years. In the early Egyptian and Indian civilizations, incense was used to drive away bad spirits and manifest the presence of gods. Native Americans burnt sage to release negative thoughts, feelings, and entities, and both the Hindu and Buddhist traditions still use incense to create an atmosphere conducive to meditation. For Roman Catholics, incense is used in many of their ceremonies to symbolize the sacredness of a person or an occasion, and to create an atmosphere that is more receptive to prayer.

With such sacred and ancient roots, the act of burning incense should be treated with respect. The Annual Spiritual Cleansing (opposite) can be a powerful cleanser and great to do after you've had a big clearout and a good clean. It can be beneficial if you've moved into a new house and want to release the energy of the previous owners or if you want to create a calm and tranquil atmosphere.

annual spiritual cleansing

You will need:

Incense (see below) and a holder
A bowl of pebbles or sand
A fan, a large feather, or a piece of card stock
Matches

1 Decide whether you are going to do a specific room or the whole house.

2 Place your incense in the holder. Light the incense so that it smoulders.

3 Take your incense to the middle of the room you've chosen and say: "I call upon the sacred powers of sage (or whatever incense you are using) to cleanse (or whatever actions they will be doing) my home. I give thanks for this help."

4 Walk around your room going into each corner with your incense. You might want to carry your bowl of pebbles or sand underneath it to prevent any bits falling onto your carpet. Or, you can stay in the center of the room and waft the smoke with your fan, feather, or piece of card in the different directions. Make sure you move the smoke above you and below you to cover all areas.

5 When you've finished, thank the herbs once again and extinguish the incense.

herbal incense for cleansing		
There are many different types of incense to choose from, but these are some of the best:		
	Basil	*Helpful for maintaining concentration, overcoming fatigue, and attracting love and wealth.*
	Bay	*Boosts energy, good for healing, protection, and attracting success.*
	Lavender	*Good for cleansing, restoring balance, and creating a peaceful atmosphere. Lavender also attracts loving energy and spirits and is good for housewarming.*
	Rosemary	*Use for stimulating, healing, and protecting. Wards off thieves, repels negativity, and brings clarity to problems. Good for love and friendship.*
	Rose geranium	*Protects the home and family, helps to restore harmony.*
	Sage	*Good for calming, healing, and cleansing, helps to bring wisdom.*
	Thyme	*Helpful for stimulating, purifying, and protecting. Good for boosting courage.*

10 things you can do right now

Keeping your home at its best can take time and energy, especially if you have just begun to adopt new habits. Commitment and patience are essential if you want to maintain your hard work, but trying one or more of the following should help you to keep up the momentum.

1   If you find that your motivation to keep on top of your household is flagging, remind yourself as to why you wanted to create a wonderful home in the first place. If it helps, you could keep pictures of homes that you admire handy to keep you in touch with what you want from your home.

2   If you're not sure when your peak times are (those times when you are most alert and energetic), keep a diary for a week. Take into account that you may be altering your energy levels by drinking caffeine or alcohol.

3   If you find that your home often reverts back to chaos, note the events that lead up to it. Is there something in your habit patterns or routine that could be altered to make it happen less often?

4   Think of something you would like to begin. This could be a new habit or routine or it could be a job, like painting a room you would like repainted. During the next New Moon (many ordinary diaries provide the New and Full Moon dates), begin your chosen task.

5   At the next Full Moon, have a look around your home and see whether there is anything you would like to get rid of. Make sure you get it out of your home before the next New Moon. The weeks between Full and New Moons are also ideal for kicking bad habits.

6 Since our natural rhythms change with the seasons, you may find that you need to alter your routine to stay in harmony with your energy levels. Think about how your lifestyle and your home function during the four seasons, then decide whether there are any changes you need to make as you enter a new season.

7 To keep in touch with the year's natural cycles, bring the season into your home. For example, in spring you could bring a bowl of bulbs into the living room, in summer fresh flowers, in autumn a bowl of shiny apples, and in winter an arrangement of pine cones.

8 Use incense to cleanse the atmosphere of the room in your home that you feel most needs it. Take a note of whether you think it has worked. Do one room each week until you have cleansed your whole home.

9 If you don't have time for a thorough spring or autumn clean in one time block, create a checklist in your notebook. Do one major task, for example washing the curtains, every week until you have completed them all. Each time you've checked off a task in your notebook, give yourself a reward.

10 Throw out three things that you don't need.

picture credits

Key: a=above, b=below, r=right, l=left, c=center.

UK Jacket bc ph Debi Treloar
Front endpapers ph Polly Wreford; Back endpapers ph Debi Treloar/Robert Elms and Christina Wilson's family home in London; 1 ph Debi Treloar/Susan Cropper's family home in London, www.63hlg.com; 2 ph Polly Wreford; 3 ph James Merrell/Janie Jackson stylist & designer; 4 ph Polly Wreford; 5, 5al,ac ph Polly Wreford; 5ar ph Debi Treloar; 6al ph David Brittain; 6l ph Jan Baldwin; 6bl ph Debi Treloar; 6bl below ph Dan Duchars; 6r-7 ph Jan Baldwin/The Meiré family home, designed by Marc Meiré; 8 ph Polly Wreford/Ros Fairman's house in London; 9 ph Catherine Gratwicke; 9al ph Polly Wreford; 9ac ph Debi Treloar; 9ar ph Dan Duchars; 10al ph Polly Wreford; 10ar & b ph Christopher Drake/John Minshaw's house in London; 11 ph Polly Wreford; 11a ph Jan Baldwin/Christopher Leach's apartment in London; 11b ph Jan Baldwin/Interior Designer Didier Gomez's apartment in Paris; 12 ph Jan Baldwin/Mona Nerenberg and Lisa Bynon's house in Sag Harbor; 13l ph David Montgomery; 13r ph Tom Leighton/Roger & Fay Oates' house in Herefordshire; 14al ph Jan Baldwin; 14cl ph Jan Baldwin/Philip Cox's house in Palm Beach designed by The Cox Group; 14cr ph Jan Baldwin; 14bl ph Debi Treloar; 14r ph Chris Tubbs; 15 ph Jan Baldwin; 15ar ph Jan Baldwin/David Davies' house in East Sussex, England; 15br ph Jan Baldwin; 16 ph Debi Treloar/Nicky Phillips' apartment in London; 17 inset ph Dan Duchars; 17 ph Debi Treloar/Clare and David Mannix-Andrews' house, Hove, East Sussex; 18a & c ph Tom Leighton; 18b-19al ph Debi Treloar/Kristiina Ratia and Jeff Gocke's family home in Norwalk, Connecticut; 19ac ph Jan Baldwin/The Meiré family home, designed by Marc Meiré; 19ar ph Catherine Gratwicke/Francesca Mills' house in London; 19bl ph Richard Learoyd/Morag Myerscough's home in Clerkenwell, London; 19bc ph Polly Wreford/Ros Fairman's house in London; 19br ph Debi Treloar/Susan Cropper's family home in London, www.63hlg.com; 20 ph James Merrell/Janie Jackson stylist & designer; 21a ph Dan Duchars; 21b ph Andrew Wood/Ian Bartlett and Christine Walsh's house in London; 22al & cl ph Polly Wreford; 22cl below ph Jan Baldwin; 22bl ph David Montgomery; 22r-23 ph Jan Baldwin/The Meiré family home, designed by Marc Meiré; 24c ph Polly Wreford/Francesca Mills' house in London; 25l ph Polly Wreford/House Stylist Clare Nash's house in London; 25r ph Polly Wreford/Glen Carwithen and Sue Miller's house in London; 26 ph Debi Treloar/Robert Elms and Christina Wilson's family home in London; 27a ph Christopher Drake/Roger & Fay Oates' house in Herefordshire; 27c ph Polly Wreford/Mary Foley's house in Connecticut; 27b ph Debi Treloar/Sarah Munro and Brian Ayling's home in London; 28al ph Polly Wreford; 28bl ph Andrew Wood/Gabriele Sanders' apartment in New York; 28r ph Tom Leighton; 29a ph Sandra Lane; 29b ph Andrew Wood/Mikko Puotila's apartment in Espoo, Finland/Interior design by Ulla Koskinen; 30 ph Andrew Wood/Alastair Hendy and John Clinch's apartment in London, designed by Alastair Hendy; 31a ph Polly Wreford/Carol Reid's apartment in Paris; 31b ph Andrew Wood/Gabriele Sanders' apartment in New York; 32-33l ph Jan Baldwin/The Meiré family home, designed by Marc Meiré; 33c ph Polly Wreford; 33r ph James Merrell/Janie Jackson stylist & designer; 34a ph Jan Baldwin/Mark Smith's home in the Cotswolds; 34b ph Melanie Eclare/Elspeth Thompson's garden in south London; 35 inset ph Chris Tubbs/Jonathan Adler and Simon Doonan's house on Shelter Island near New York/designed by Schefer Design; 35 ph Jan Baldwin; 36 ph Simon Upton/Zara Colchester's house in London; 37a ph Christopher Drake/Vivien Lawrence, Interior Designer in London; 37b ph Debi Treloar/Family home in London of Paul Balland and Jane Wadham of jwflowers.com; 38 ph Andrew Wood/Mikko Puotila's apartment in Espoo, Finland/Interior design by Ulla Koskinen; 39a ph Chris Everard/Interior Designer Ann Boyd's own apartment in London; 39b ph Debi Treloar/Nicky Phillips' apartment in London; 40 ph Debi Treloar/Robert Elms and Christina Wilson's family home in London; 41a ph Debi Treloar/ Susan Cropper's family home in London, www.63hlg.com; 41bl

ph Caroline Arber/Emma Bowman Interior Design/All work by Caroline Zoob; 41bc ph Debi Treloar/An apartment in London by Malin Iovino Design; 41br ph Debi Treloar/Ben Johns and Deb Waterman Johns' house in Georgetown; 42al & ac ph Polly Wreford; 42r ph Polly Wreford/Lena Proudlock's house in Gloucestershire; 42b ph Dan Duchars; 43l ph Jan Baldwin/Sophie Eadie's family home in London; 43ar ph Henry Bourne; 43cr ph Debi Treloar/ Robert Elms and Christina Wilson's family home in London; 43br ph Chris Everard; 44 ph Debi Treloar; 45l ph Jan Baldwin; 45ar ph Polly Wreford; 45cr ph Andrew Wood/Gabriele Sanders' apartment in New York; 45br ph Debi Treloar; 46al ph Alan Williams; 46cl & bcl ph Polly Wreford; 46bl ph Andrew Wood/Gabriele Sanders' apartment in New York; 46r-47 ph Andrew Wood/Mikko Puotila's apartment in Espoo, Finland/Interior design by Ulla Koskinen; 48 ph Dan Duchars; 49a ph Andrew Wood; 49c ph Dan Duchars; 49b ph Tom Leighton; 50 ph Polly Wreford; 51bl ph Debi Treloar; 51bc ph Jan Baldwin; 51br ph Polly Wreford; 52al ph Polly Wreford/Francesca Mills' house in London; 52c ph David Brittain; 52br ph Polly Wreford/Karen Nicol and Peter Clark's home in London; 53al ph Catherine Gratwicke; 53c & br ph Caroline Arber; 54 ph Debi Treloar/Nicky Phillips' apartment in London; 55a ph Caroline Arber; 55b ph Dan Duchars; 56a ph Catherine Gratwicke; 56b ph Catherine Gratwicke/Rose Hammick's home in London; 57a ph Tom Leighton; 57b ph Caroline Arber; 58ar ph Andrew Wood; 58br ph Andrew Wood; 58b ph Polly Wreford; 59 ph Catherine Gratwicke/House Stylist Clare Nash's home in London; 60 ph Debi Treloar/Mark and Sally of Baileys Home & Garden's house in Herefordshire; 61a ph Polly Wreford; 61b ph Catherine Gratwicke; 62l ph Debi Treloar; 62ar ph Catherine Gratwicke/Francesca Mills' house in London; 62br ph Andrew Wood; 63 ph Polly Wreford; 64 ph Debi Treloar/Imogen Chappel's home in Suffolk; 65 ph Debi Treloar/Robert Elms and Christina Wilson's family home in London; 65 inset ph James Merrell; 66ar ph David Brittain; 66br ph Andrew Wood; 66c ph Tom Leighton; 67 ph Dan Duchars; 68 ph Debi Treloar/Family home in Bankside, London; 69a ph Sandra Lane; 69c ph James Merrell; 69b ph Caroline Arber; 70r ph Debi Treloar/ Family home in London of Paul Balland and Jane Wadham of jwflowers.com; 70l ph Debi Treloar/ Kristiina Ratia and Jeff Gocke's family home in Norwalk, Connecticut; 71 ph Jan Baldwin/ Sophie Eadie's family home in London; 72ar ph David Brittain; 72c ph Jan Baldwin; 72b ph James Merrell; 73l ph David Montgomery; 73ar-br ph Caroline Arber; 74 ph Andrew Wood/House in London designed by Guy Stansfeld; 75a & c ph Polly Wreford; 75b ph Debi Treloar; 76 ph Jan Baldwin/Peter and Nicole Dawes' apartment/Designed by Mullman Seidman Architects; 77a ph Peter Cassidy; 77b ph Chris Tubbs/Nickerson-Wakefield house in upstate New York/Designed by anderson architects; 78 ph Ray Main; 79l ph Andrew Wood; 79ar & br ph Debi Treloar; 79cr ph David Montgomery; 80al ph Polly Wreford; 80cl ph Debi Treloar/Dominique Coughlin's apartment in London; 80cl below ph David Brittain; 80bl ph Debi Treloar; 80r & 81 ph Polly Wreford/Kimberley Watson's house in London; 82 ph Jan Baldwin/Family home in Parsons Green London/Architecture by Nicholas Helm and Yasuyuki Fukuda (architectural assistant) of Helm Architects; 83 ph Polly Wreford; 84r ph Polly Wreford; 84l ph Jan Baldwin; 85 ph David Montgomery; 86 ph James Merrell; 86 inset ph Tom Leighton; 87a ph Polly Wreford; 87c ph Jan Baldwin; 87b ph Chris Everard/Jonathan Wilson's apartment in London; 88al & ar, cl ph Polly Wreford; 88acl & r ph Debi Treloar/Home of Studio Aandacht/Designed by Ben Lambers; 88bl ph Debi Treloar/Debi Treloar's family home in northwest London; 88br ph Polly Wreford/Louise Jackson's house in London; 89 ph Debi Treloar/Debi Treloar's family home in northwest London; 90 ph Ray Main; 90al ph Ray Main/Loft in London designed by Nico Rensch; 90ar ph Andrew Wood/Christer Wallensteen's apartment in Stockholm, Sweden; 91 ph Jan Baldwin/Interior Designer Didier Gomez's apartment in Paris; 92 ph Jan Baldwin; 92ar ph Ray Main/The contemplative space of Greville Worthington; 92br ph Polly Wreford/Kimberley Watson's house in London; 93-93ar ph Polly Wreford; 93br ph Debi Treloar; 94a ph Caroline Arber; 94b ph David Montgomery; 95 ph William Lingwood; 95a ph Caroline Arber/Rosanna Dickinson's home in London; 95b ph David Montgomery; 96a ph Polly

126

Wreford; **97** ph Dan Duchars; **98** ph Chris Tubbs; **98a** ph Polly Wreford; **98b** ph Dan Duchars; **99** ph Polly Wreford; **100** ph Debi Treloar/Susan Cropper's family home in London, www.63hlg.com; **101** ph Daniel Farmer; **101l** ph Emma Lee; **101r–102** ph Polly Wreford; **103** ph Simon Upton/Residence in Highlands, North Carolina/Designed by Nancy Braithwaite Interiors; **104** ph Jan Baldwin/Claire Haithwaite and Dean Maryon's home in Amsterdam; **105a** ph Dan Duchars; **105b** ph Debi Treloar/Catherine Chermayeff and Jonathan David's family home in New York/Designed by Asfour Guzy Architects; **106–107** ph Polly Wreford; **107l** Louise Jackson's house in London; **108** ph Tom Leighton; **109** ph Jan Baldwin/Michael D'Souza of Mufti; **109 inset** ph James Merrell; **110a** ph Debi Treloar; **110b** ph Caroline Arber; **111** ph Polly Wreford/Kimberley Watson's house in London; **112** ph Debi Treloar/Clare and David Mannix-Andrews' house; **113a** ph David Montgomery; **113b** ph Polly Wreford; **114al** ph James Merrell; **114cl** ph Debi Treloar; **114cl below** ph Christopher Drake; **114bl** ph Andrew Wood/Alastair Hendy and John Clinch's apartment in London, designed by Alastair Hendy; **114r–115** ph Polly Wreford/Marie-Hélène de Taillac's pied-à-terre in Paris; **116** ph Debi Treloar/Susan Cropper's family home in London, www.63hlg.com; **116 inset** ph James Merrell; **117** ph Polly Wreford; **118** ph Debi Treloar; **118a** ph Chris Tubbs; **118b** ph Henry Bourne; **119a** ph Jan Baldwin/Camp Kent/Designed by Alexandra Champalimaud; **119b** ph Andrew Wood/Gabriele Sanders' apartment in New York; **120** ph Debi Treloar/Robert Elms and Christina Wilson's family home in London; **121a** ph Andrew Wood/Apartment in London designed by Hogarth Architects (previously Littman Goddard Hogarth Architects); **121bl** ph Debi Treloar; **121bc** ph David Brittain; **121br** ph Chris Everard/Programmable house in London designed by d-squared; **122–123** ph Polly Wreford; **122a** ph David Montgomery; **122b–123 chart** ph Caroline Arber; **124** ph Debi Treloar; **125l** ph Chris Tubbs; **125ar** ph Polly Wreford; **125cr & br** ph James Merrell; **126–127** ph Tom Leighton; **128** ph Debi Treloar.

business credits

Alexandra Champalimaud & Associates Inc
One Union Square West, #603
New York, NY 10003
t. +1 212 807 8869
f. +1 212 807 1742
www.alexchamp.com
Pages 119a

anderson architects
555 West 25th Street
New York, NY 10001
t. +1 212 620 0996
f. +1 212 620 5299
e.info@andersonarch.com
www.andersonarch.com
Pages 77b

Baileys Home & Garden
The Engine Shed
Station Approach
Ross-on-Wye
Herefordshire HR9 7BW, UK
t. +44 1989 563015
sales@baileys-home-garden.co.uk
www.baileyshomeandgarden.com
Pages 60

Emma Bowman Interior Design
t. +44 20 7622 2592
emmabowman@yahoo.co.uk
Pages 41bl

Ann Boyd Design Ltd
33 Elystan Place
London SW3 3NT, UK
t. +44 20 7591 0202
f. +44 20 7591 0404
Pages 39a

Nancy Braithwaite Interiors
2300 Peachtree Road
Suite C101
Atlanta, Georgia 30309
Pages 103

Lisa Bynon Garden Design
PO Box 897
Sag Harbor
New York 11963
t. +1 631 725 4680
Pages 12

Imogen Chappel
t. +44 7803 156 081
Pages 64

Zara Colchester
Writer
20 Frewen Road
London SW18 3LP, UK
Pages 36

The Cox Group
Architects and Planners
204 Clarence Street
Sydney 2000
Australia
t. +61 2 9267 9599
f. +61 2 9264 5844
www.cox.com.au
Pages 14cl

Susan Cropper
www.63hlg.com
Pages 1, 19br, 41a, 100, 116

d-squared design
6b Blackbird Yard
Ravenscroft Street
London E2 7RP, UK
t. +44 20 7739 2632
f. +44 20 7739 2633
dsquared@globalnet.co.uk
Pages 121br

Ory Gomez, Didier Gomez
Interior Designer
15 rue Henri Heine
75016 Paris
France
t. +33 01 44 30 8823
f. +33 01 45 25 1816
orygomez@free.fr
Pages 11b, 91

Asfour Guzy Architects
594 Broadway
New York, NY 10012
t. +1 212 334 9350
Pages 104b

Helm Architects
2 Montagu Row
London W1U 6DX, UK
t. +44 20 7224 1884
f. +44 20 7224 1885
nh@helmarchitects.com
Pages 82

Alastair Hendy
Food Writer, Art Director, & Designer
f. +44 20 739 6040
Pages 30, 114bl

Hogarth Architects
61 Courtfield Gardens
London SW5 0NQ, UK
t. +44 20 7565 8366
www.hogartharchitects.co.uk
Pages 121a

Vivien Lawrence Interior Design
Interior Designer of private homes—any project from start to finish, small or large.
London, UK
t. +44 20 8209 0058/0562
vl-interiordesign@cwcom.net
Pages 37a

Malin Iovino Design
t/f. +44 20 7252 3542
m. +44 7956 326122
iovino@btconnect.com
Pages 41bc

Janie Jackson/Parma Lilac
+ 44 20 7912 0882
Children's nursery furnishings and accessories
Pages 3, 20, 33r

Jacksons
5 All Saints Road
London W11 1HA, UK
t. +44 20 7792 8336
Pages 88br, 107l

jwflowers.com
Unit E8 & 9
1–45 Durham Street
London SE11 5JH, UK
t. +44 20 7735 7771
f. +44 20 7735 2011
jane@jwflowers.com
www.jwflowers.com
Pages 37b, 70r

Christopher Leach Design Ltd
Interior Designer
m. +44 7765 255566
mail@christopherleach.com
Pages 11a

Francesca Mills
Designer/Stylist
t. +44 20 7733 9193
Pages 19ar, 24c, 52al, 62ar

John Minshaw Designs Ltd
17 Upper Wimpole Street
London W1H 6LU, UK
t. +44 20 7258 5777
f. +44 20 7486 6777
enquiries@johnminshawdesigns.com
Pages 10ar–b

Mufti
789 Fulham Road
London SW6 5HA, UK
t. +44 20 7610 9123
f. +44 20 7384 2050
www.mufti.co.uk
Pages 109

Mona Nerenberg
Bloom
43 Madison Street
Sag Harbor
New York 11963
t. +1 631 725 4680
Pages 12

Roger & Fay Oates
The Long Barn
Eastnor, Ledbury
Herefordshire HR8 1EL, UK
t. +44 1531 632718
www.rogeroates.co.uk
Flooring, plates, place mats & glassware by Roger Oates
Pages 13r, 27a

Kristiina Ratia Designs
t. +1 203 852 0027
Pages 18b–19al, 70l

Nico Rensch Architeam
t. +44 7711 412898
Pages 90al

Schefer Design
David Schefer & Eve-Lynn Schoenstein
41 Union Square West, No 1427
New York, NY 10003
t. +1 212 691 9097
f. +1 212 691 9520
scheferdesign@mindspring.com
www.scheferdesign.com
Pages 35 inset

Guy Stansfeld
t. +44 20 8962 8666
Pages 74

Studio Aandacht
Art direction & interior production
ben.lambers@studioaandacht.nl
www.studioaandacht.nl
Pages 88acl–r

Wallensteen & Co ab
Architect & Design Consultants
Floragatan 11
114 31 Stockholm
Sweden
t/f. +46 8 210151
m. +46 70 7203117
wallensteen@chello.se
Pages 90ar

Christina Wilson
Interiors Stylist
christinawilson@btopenworld.com
Pages 26, 40, 43cr, 65, 120, back endpapers

Caroline Zoob
Textile Artist and interior design
For commissions:
t. +44 1273 479274
Pages 41bl

index